Baking Breakfast

Delicious, Wholesome Muffins, Breads and Cakes Inspired by Three Generations of Family Cooking

Jill Berkowitz Provan

Baking Breakfast: Delicious, Wholesome Muffins, Breads and Cakes Inspired by Three Generations of Family Cooking

Third Impression, 2015
www.baking-breakfast.com

Designed by Jessica Y Lee

Library of Congress Control Number: 2014912141
ISBN: 978-0-9912372-0-3

COOKING / Courses & Dishes / Breakfast

This book is printed in the United States of America.

Baking Breakfast is dedicated with love to my husband, Keith G. Provan (1947–2014), the biggest fan of my baking, who eagerly sampled every recipe in this book; to my father, Leonard Berkowitz (1917–1991); and my mother, Thelma Gruber Berkowitz (1924–2012), who couldn't wait to see this book done.

Contents

Introduction

THE BERKOWITZ FAMILY

Food was important in Harry and Frances Berkowitz's house, a family affair shared with any of their children's friends who happened to be around at meal time, and aunts and cousins and nieces, who filled the house each Friday night to eat dinner and play the Russian card game Durak ("the fool").

Frances, a barely five-feet-tall bundle of energy, was welcoming and relaxed. She did, however, maintain an orderly home and encouraged responsibility. A weekly job list was taped to the inside door of a kitchen cabinet and everyone had a part in keeping the kitchen functioning. (All except George, who usually had a date or some other engagement on the nights when it was his turn to wash the dishes.) Responsibilities didn't stop in the home. They included working at Harry's grocery store, Legal Cash Market, in Boston's Inman Square. Harry's children and grandchildren all harbor memories of exploring the meat locker filled with hanging animal carcasses, and, when allowed, freely grabbing a treat from the shelves of food. My mainstay was a small, rectangular box of Cheez-Its, which I toted around the store by a purse-style string.

After a long week at Legal's, Harry proudly escorted Frances, whom he called "my girl," and their five children—in order of birth: Leonard, George, Ethel, Stanley, and Donald—out to dinner. Each Sunday they walked from their Mattapan home down the street to their favorite Chinese restaurant. That changed when Frances decided it was time to move the family to the suburbs. When the perfect home went on sale in Newton, she hastily purchased it without consulting Harry. They moved into the new house, and Harry did not talk to Frances for one month—quite an ordeal for a man whose first action when he came home from work late at night was to embrace his wife, lift her up, and exclaim, "How's my girl?"

I remember the back door that my grandfather walked through into this house each night, because it opened onto a screened porch—and what treasures that porch held! In winter it served as a second refrigerator, laden with pots of beans and meat and potato dumplings (tzimmes), among other mouth-watering delights. There were never enough of those sticky, sweet dumplings. I've never tasted them anywhere else; or, if I have, the experience was flushed away by the memory of my grandmother's incomparable ones.

When the extended family grew larger, we spent holidays at my Aunt Ethel and Uncle Oscar's large home in Beverly, Massachusetts. My cousins, aunts, uncles, and Grammy and Granddaddy drove the 45 minutes for a daylong celebration. Of course, the focus of the festivities was food – and could Ethel cook! There was so much variety and creativity: spare ribs, baked Alaska, and turkey with three different dressings. Years later, early in our marriage, my husband Keith and I moved to Boston for a few years. Ethel often invited us to dinner. "That was the first time I ever had a meal with more than one main course," Keith says, still marveling at Ethel's concoctions 35 years later.

While the Berkowitz children loved food, most were content to eat what their mother made. Only Leonard exhibited early signs of culinary curiosity. When he arrived home from working at the market, and passed through the kitchen, with his mother's dinner simmering on the stove, he would loom over the pots and add "a dash of this and a dash of that." This habit continued throughout his life. I remember one time, as a teenager, when my sisters, Diane and Cindy, my mother and I sat down to a much-anticipated pot of my mother's tomato sauce. My mother took one bite, gagged slightly, and turned to my father with daggers in her eyes: "Leonard!" she said sternly. He had added too much red pepper and was the only one who ended up being able to eat the meal.

Like her siblings, Ethel did not start cooking until she married and left home. Later in life she began to draw, paint, and sculpt, but cooking was her first creative outlet. No recipe was too difficult or too odd. She bought a big freezer for the basement and kept it filled. Everyone who visited was happy to help empty it.

George was the only one to make cooking a career. In 1950 he opened a fish market adjacent to his father's grocery, where he fried fish on Fridays for the Catholics in the neighborhood. Julia Child was living in Cambridge at the time and bought all her fish from George. In 1968, when he opened Legal Sea Foods Restaurant next to his shop, on the site of Legal Cash Market, Child created the signature recipe for the coleslaw that accompanied every meal. Legal Sea Foods has become a Boston institution, and now, six decades later, the restaurant has more than 35 locations populating the Eastern Seaboard, as well as an online fish market and retail product line. For my cousin Roger Berkowitz, who took over as CEO and president of Legal Sea Foods in 1992, eating good food isn't just an essential part of life; it's his livelihood.

My father Leonard also made a career for himself in the food-service industry. He was the author of *Meat Source: A Newsletter for the Foodservice Industry Covering Meats, Fish and Poultry*, which was published from 1986 through 1988. He also taught meat science at Florida International University's hospitality management school, where he was known as Mister Meat. The older he got, the more he cooked.

On weekends he would spend hours in the kitchen preparing a roast: tenderly patting the prime rib dry with paper towels, concocting the perfect marinade, and calibrating the oven. Dad watched over the meat like a mother hen, adjusting the temperature at the optimal time for maximum juiciness. Sometimes I assisted him, sharing his cigarettes and Scotch. I did write down some of his recipes, but he usually made things up as he went; I had to pressure him for approximate measurements. Unfortunately, I never recorded the many marinades with which he embellished all of his roasts. And I have rarely attempted to duplicate them. On those few occasions when I have, I couldn't match the texture of the glazes, the intense flavors of soy sauce, herbs, vermouth, and sugar.

Harry and Frances instilled in their children a love of food and cooking. For Leonard, George, Ethel, Stanley, and Donald, shopping for ingredients and preparing, serving, and eating food with friends and loved ones were the highlights of their days. Whenever I do the same, I find myself conjuring memories of these wonderful people and the meals they shared.

THE GRUBER FAMILY

I inherited my grandma Sophie Gruber's rolling pin. She used it daily to make cinnamon rolls, strudels, and lemon meringue and fruit pies. For her children—Stanley, Roslyn, Thelma, and Sylvia—these delicacies were legend. The three daughters, especially Roslyn, helped Sophie bake while growing up, and then made her dinner recipes themselves when they raised their families. Unfortunately, Sophie's pastry recipes were not passed on to the next generation. She never wrote anything down and never measured. She would show you how to roll out the dough or whip up a meringue, but when you asked, "How much of this?" or "How much of that?" she would reply with some consternation: "Well, until it's the right consistency," or, "Until it tastes right." Sophie was an intuitive cook who understood how ingredients fit together. The recipes might be gone but her children's memories of their mother's kitchen were not. Sylvia remembers:

Sophie's baking was extraordinary. I wish I had the recipe for her lemon meringue pie, which was phenomenal. I remember that she grated lemon skin into the mixture and saved unused egg whites for a week, which made the topping enormous. She always made pies in huge sizes. When one came out of the oven, it was really significant, like a ship had landed on the kitchen counter!

Sophie's home meant a lot to her. She was an immigrant who came to the United States at age five, and endured relative poverty growing up. Sophie lived with her older sister and her sister's mean husband, and had to care for their many children. She never forgot what it was like to be persecuted as a child in Russia and to live in poverty. When she married and got a lovely apartment in Newton, it meant the world to her.

The kitchen held special power. It went through many transformations, but the back room, off the kitchen, always held the icebox. When I was five or six, in the mid 1930s, ice was delivered twice a week. Later, the icebox was replaced with a snazzy white GE electric refrigerator, which Sophie adored.

The first stove we had was the old-fashioned kind with the gas burners below the broiler, which was beneath the high oven. I can still smell the lamb chops broiling. We had them frequently—they were very cheap, and everyone loved them. We ate the chops with baked potatoes (with heavenly burnt skins) and Le Sueur peas from a can.

But Sophie never skimped in the kitchen. We had great fresh vegetables and fruit; Sophie played cards every day and on the way home she often stopped for provisions at a farm on Chestnut Hill Avenue in Brighton. Our meat was delivered from Brookline, where there was a Jewish butcher called Handler's. Mother would get on the phone with Pauline, the secretary, and ask if she would mind going next door to the Jewish bakery to get some loaves of good pumpernickel bread to go along with the delivery. One morning Thelma and I were in bed and overheard Sophie say to Pauline, "Tell me, Pauline, do you have a fresh tongue?" Thelma and I screamed with laughter at the double meaning.

Feeding a family of six was no small challenge, and Sophie spent many hours in the kitchen. I can still see her in her chenille bathrobe and hair net, rousing the household early in the morning, preparing for a day of cooking.

THE NEXT GENERATION

As soon as my children, Alexander and Olivia, could sit on the kitchen stool without falling off, they became my baking sous chefs. Measuring and combining ingredients were among their favorite activities. They took pride in mastering the Kitchen Aid standing mixer despite my obsessive instructions about kitchen safety: "Make sure the mixer is in off mode when you plug it in. Unplug it as soon as you finish mixing. Don't get your hands near the beater when the mixer is on. Be careful when you put a pan in the preheated oven. Be careful when you take the pan out of the oven." And so on. It's a wonder they lasted. I often thought they only stuck around to lick the batter—and I guess that was worth enduring my warnings.

Olivia started off cooking in her own miniature kitchen. By age five, she was often busy expanding her repertoire, which came to include pigs in a blanket (hot dogs encased in dough), scrambled eggs, and grilled cheese sandwiches. Eventually she began baking without me, contributing to the supply of fresh muffins and coffee cakes the family feasted on each morning before leaving for school and work.

When Olivia and Alexander left home for college, cooking and eating became a part of their social lives. Each of them gained recognition in their social circles as cooks and bakers. These days their inventions often outshine my own. When Alexander is home for holidays, Keith and I tease him about the extravagant lunches he prepares: toast piled with slivers of goat cheese, strips of smoked salmon, and wedges of tomato, meticulously adorned with capers, olive oil, and crushed red pepper. We provide the full fridge, and he rewards us with brussel sprouts in bacon balsamic reduction, and Oaxaca-style shrimp tacos. For Olivia's part, coming home often means trying out a recipe for lemon scented ricotta on garlic toast with honey or soaked duck Vietnamese spring rolls with two dipping sauces with Keith and myself acting as her test subjects.

It is a rare descendent of either Harry and Frances Berkowitz or Harry and Sophie Gruber who can pass by a bakery or meat-and-cheese shop without pausing to look longingly through the window, or going inside to absorb the aromas—and usually buy a bag full of whatever is offered.

A HOME BAKER'S EVOLUTION

I spent much of my childhood drooling over pictures of cakes in magazines, pitting the desire to eat against the desire to be svelte—a habit I continue to this day.

Cooking is functional and rewarding, but my passion has always been baking, a therapy for anything that ails me. Sometimes I think I had children in order to consistently empty my freezer of excess breakfast breads. After the children left home for college, I dispensed baked goods at work. As I biked the ten miles to the Tucson Museum of Art, where I was the librarian, I looked forward to dropping off muffins with friends along the way. So my job also acted as a way of keeping my freezer from exploding. And even while working as a librarian and editor, I couldn't resist taking on occasional baking catering jobs, which meant camping out in the kitchen till midnight, whipping up chocolate chestnut tortes and pumpkin muffins.

Growing up eating wonderful food made with the best-quality ingredients has shaped my life. I am passionate about the cooking process and appreciate being able to do it well. I love everything about it: shopping for the food, handling fruits and vegetables, sautéing onions, and luxuriating in the scents of a perfectly executed meal.

Baking has become my inheritance, a connection to the world of food germinated generations ago by my family, and to the intimate experiences and memories that bind family and friends. Some years after Grammy's death at 99, Aunt Ethel gave me a small, handwritten, 3-ring binder with my grandmother's recipes. As I pored over the recipes (four for rugelach, five for noodle pudding, etc.), I was inspired to do what I had talked about for years: compile my own baking cookbook.

In **Baking Breakfast**, I have put my passion to work. I have created recipes, and updated the traditional ingredients of my parents and grandparents by adding healthy ingredients that have only recently become widely available, such as whole wheat flour, ground nuts, and fresh yogurt. The result is delicious, wholesome breakfast breads, muffins and cakes.

I like watching people eat what I have baked. I even like imagining them bestowing compliments on my creations when I'm not around. Most of all, though, I like to lick the bowl. So here's to happy licking.

The Lists

My Ten Rules for Baking

1. Whatever you're baking must taste good.

2. It should be easy to make. All recipes are simpler when you follow these steps. Before making a recipe, read it from beginning to end. Then put everything you need to use (mise en place) on the counter. After finishing with each ingredient, either set it aside or return it to the shelf.

3. The baked good should be made from fresh, local ingredients (whenever possible). Flour is a great example. The quality of flour can make or break a recipe. A lot of flour in supermarkets is stale. All-purpose flour that is unbleached has a shelf life of about eight months. After that the fat in the flour will start to go rancid. Conventional bleached flour will keep for an almost unlimited period without turning, though it will eventually dry out. The oily, corned flavored germ of ground corn meal is often removed for preservation. When it is not, the oil goes rancid after a few weeks on the shelf. Use the best ingredients.

4. Unless directed otherwise, never over-mix the batter for either muffins or quick breads. Flour should not be beaten or whipped when baking something sweet. Instead, mix it quickly with a rubber spatula or wood spoon just until the flour is not visible. (Quick breads use chemical leavening, such as baking soda or baking powder, rather than yeast. They can be either sweet or savory.) In general, the process for making them is to: first, mix the dry ingredients; second, mix the wet ingredients; briefly combine the dry and wet; and bake.

5. Avoid opening the oven too often when checking for doneness. However, it may be necessary to bake longer or shorter than my recommended times. All ovens are different, and my times are based on my own oven.

If you use a convection oven for baking, it is important to follow a few guidelines. Reduce the temperature listed on the recipe by 25° F (4° C). Many ovens with convection features do this automatically. Also, check the items for doneness 10 minutes before the recipe says. Smaller cakes bake faster and larger may take longer.

6. Do not refrigerate or freeze breakfast muffins or breads that will be consumed within 48 hours. The exception is if the weather is warm and the house is hot. For storing, I wrap the cooled product tightly in plastic wrap. If freezing, I also cover with foil that I label with name and date. (Optional: In addition, place wrapped product in a plastic bag.)

7. The best way to refresh your muffins, breads, and tea cakes is to bake them, defrosted and uncovered, for 5-10 minutes in an oven preheated to 300-350° F (150-185° C).

8. Follow some guidelines when baking with fruit. I have described a few fruits common in baking. Use them as a basis for trying other fruits.

Apples. Many varieties of apples can be used for baking. Some of the commonly available ones are: the sweet Braeburn, Crispin and Rome; the tart Granny Smith, Ida Red and Northern Spy; and the sweet-tart Fuji, Honeycrisp, Jonathan, Jonagold and Winesap.

Pears. There are also many types of pears good for cooking. These include the easy-to-find Bartlett, Comice, Bosc and D'Anjou.

Berries. (Rinse and dry fresh berries.) To avoid their sinking to the bottom of a product, and to keep them dispersed throughout the cake, lightly dust with 1-3 teaspoons flour just before mixing into the batter. Be careful not to over-dust. This may cause them to be gummy.

Frozen fruit. (When fresh fruit is unavailable, use frozen.) Do not defrost. Instead, just prior to using, quickly rinse in a colander with water, and dry. This gets rid of any frost, which tends to absorb unwanted odors. When adding the fruit to the batter, stir gently, to avoid breaking up the berries. Use smaller berries whenever possible.

9. Use spices generously. Spices enhance the flavor of a product. I often combine: 2 teaspoons cinnamon, ¼ teaspoon ground cloves, and 1 teaspoon each nutmeg, coriander and cardamom and add to the batter.

10. Avoid accidents with your standing mixer. Unplug the mixer whenever you scrape down the sides of the bowl, insert or remove an attachment.

Before You Begin: Pans, Ovens, and Cooling

Unless otherwise noted, follow these basic steps for preparing pans, baking, and cooling in all recipes.

1. Place the oven rack in the middle position. Lightly butter and flour the bottom and sides of the pan(s), knocking out excess flour, or place muffin cups in the muffin tin.

2. Removing bread from the pan. Cool in pan on a rack for 20 minutes. Run a butter knife between the edges of the bread and the pan. Place the cooling rack on top of the pan. Hold the two together while turning both over. Place the rack on the counter and remove the pan from the bread. If the bread sticks, gently tap the bottom of the pan and, if necessary, pull it loose with the butter knife. Turn the bread right side up and cool completely on rack.

3. Removing a bundt cake from a pan. Cool in pan on a rack for 20 minutes. Run a butter knife between the edges of the cake and pan, then unhinge and remove the ring. Keep cake on the bottom of the pan. To remove muffins and mini-loaves, loosen the loaves with a butter knife around the edges. Place the cooling rack on top of pan. Hold the two together. Turn both over. Place the cooling rack on the counter and lift the pan.

4. Removing muffins from pan. Cool in pan on rack for 20 minutes. Place the cooling rack on top of the pan. Hold the two together and flip. Turn the muffins right side up and cool completely on rack.

5. I use the terms jumbo, standard-size, and miniature for sizes of muffins. The cup sizes are approximately 3-½ inches, 2-½ inches, and 2 inches.

Useful Kitchen Tools

Nut grinder, manual with coarse and fine settings

Glass measuring cups of varying sizes

Nesting measuring cups, 1 or 2 sets (with measurement indicators that will not wear off)

Measuring spoons, 2 sets (with ⅛ teaspoon, ⅓ teaspoon, plus standard sizes)

Standing mixer, with 2 bowls (If possible, invest in a good one. It can last a lifetime and cut your baking time in half.)

Flour sifter (that is easy to clean and dry, and is rust-proof)

Pans. Invest in good pans. The quality of a pan has a direct effect on the quality of your product. Pan sizes vary. Use these dimensions as guidelines.

Bundt pan, 10 cup
Cookie sheet pans, 2 (same as a sheet pan without sides)
Loaf pans, 2 (8-½ x 4-½ x 2-¾ inches)
Mini-loaf pans, 4 (5-½ x 3 x 2 inches)
Muffin tin, 12 cup (medium)
Muffin tin, 6 cup (large)
Muffin tin, 24 or 36 cup (miniature)
Sheet pan, 1 (¾ size at 15 x 21 inches or half size at 18 x 13 inches) (with 1-inch sides sloping in toward the bottom)
Spring form pan (8 or 9 x 3 inches)
Square brownie pan (8 x 8 x 2 or 9 x 9 x 2 inches)

Spatulas, 1 durable and slightly flexible for scraping batter out of a mixing bowl; and 1 medium offset for pushing batter around evenly and smoothly

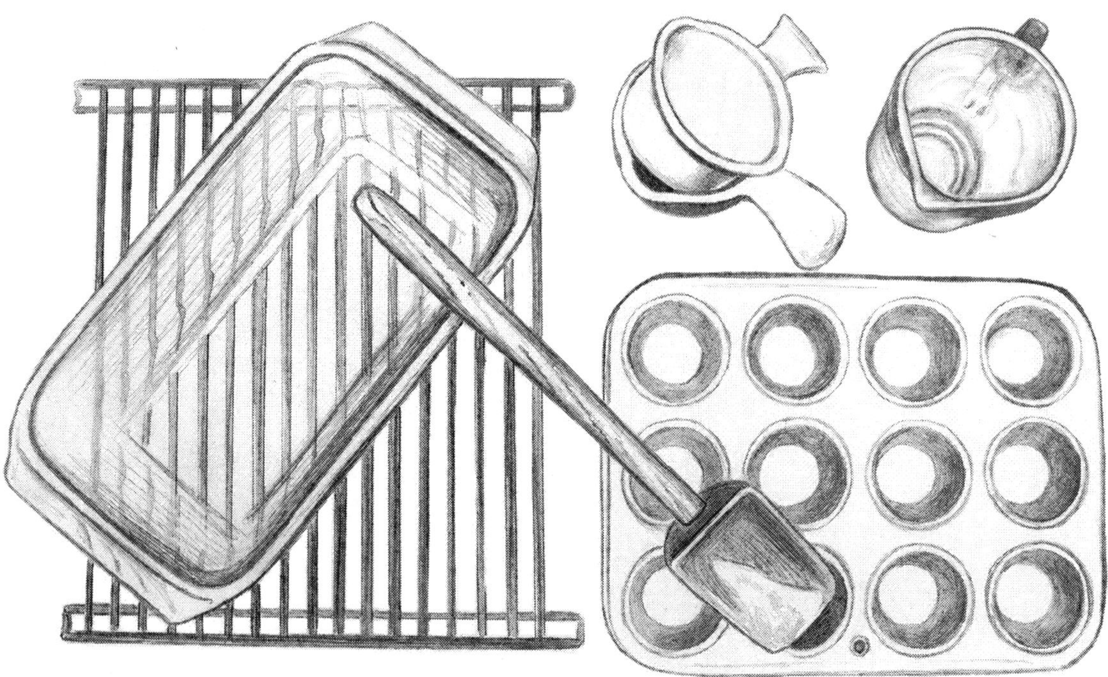

Cooling racks, 2

Ceramic-coating cookware. Ceramic-coated cookware has a chemical-free coating. The ceramic powder that is used in the coating is natural. Another benefit of ceramic-coated cookware is that it can be used for years without having any stains or other discoloration from food. In addition, it is easy to clean.

Food processor

Grater, manual

Paper muffin cup inserts

Parchment paper. Makes 9 x 5-inch loaf and mini-loaf pans easy to clean. Lightly butter and flour the pan. Snugly line the pan with parchment paper, pressing pleats flat. Lightly flour.

Pastry cutter

Cutting board (large for chopping)

Santoku knife (7-inch) for chopping

Wood spoon (medium) for stirring

Whisk. A cooking utensil used to incorporate air into a mixture or to blend ingredients smooth. Most have a long, slender handle with a number of wire loops joined at the end. (Wires are generally metal or plastic. I have three, two metal and one plastic. One metal is an attachment for my standing mixer and the plastic is for use with nonstick cookware.)

Rolling pin. None of my recipes requires one, but it should be in a baker's kitchen.

Sixteen Quickest Recipes

Apple Cereal Muffins

Banana Bread, Basic

Buttermilk Biscuits with Shredded Cheese and Herb

Cappuccino Honey Chip Muffins

Gluten-Free Buttermilk Biscuits with Shredded Cheese and Herb

Gluten-Free Mesquite Almond Tea Cake

Gluten-Free Olive Oil and Orange Corn Cake

Maple Syrup Bread

Mesquite Almond Tea Cake

Peanut Butter Chip Muffins

Pecan Sour Cream Dream Cake

Pumpkin Granola Muffins

Pumpkin Oatmeal Double Streusel Muffins

Raisin Bran Muffins

Drop Scones with Lemon, Poppyseeds, Jam, and Walnuts

Sour Cream Coffee Cake

Eight Recipes with Batter That Can Be Made Ahead

The batter for these recipes can be used immediately or kept covered and refrigerated for up to 2 days before baking.

Apple Cereal Muffins

Buttermilk Biscuits with Shredded Cheese and Herb

Carrot Bran Muffins

Chuck's Chocolate Chip Peanut Butter Oatmeal Cookies

Gluten-Free Buttermilk Biscuits with Shredded Cheese and Herb

Gluten-Free Drop Scones with Lemon, Poppyseeds, Jam, and Walnuts

Raisin Bran Muffins

Drop Scones with Lemon, Poppyseeds, Jam, and Walnuts

Six Gluten-Free Recipes

Gluten-Free Buttermilk Biscuits with Shredded Cheese and Herb

Gluten-Free Granola Breakfast Bars

Gluten-Free Mesquite Almond Tea Cake

Gluten-Free Nutty Granola

Gluten-Free Olive Oil and Orange Corn Cake

Gluten-Free Drop Scones with Lemon, Poppyseeds, Jam, and Walnuts

Traditional Recipes

Apple Cereal Muffins

EVER WONDER WHAT TO DO with Raisin Bran cereal, other than eat it with milk? In the "old days," it was near impossible to find a cold breakfast cereal that was not sugar-laden and overly processed. No longer. With the availability of healthier cereals, over the years I modified this familiar recipe until I arrived at an up-to-date, quick and delicious muffin that is more nutritious than its predecessors. These muffins are best the day or the day after they are made. To keep tasty, wrap each in plastic and store at room temperature. The batter can be used immediately or kept refrigerated for up to 2 days.

For the Muffins

1-¾ cups healthy raisin bran cereal
½ cup whole wheat pastry flour
¾ cup unbleached all-purpose flour
½ cup plus 2 tablespoons white sugar
1-¼ teaspoons baking soda
¼ teaspoon sea salt
¼ cup vegetable oil
¾ cup low-fat buttermilk
1 large-extra large egg
½ cup finely chopped apple

Apple Nut Topping

2 tablespoons plus 1-½ teaspoons unsalted butter, melted
1 tablespoon plus 1-½ teaspoons packed light brown sugar
¼ cup chopped pecans or walnuts
¼ cup finely-chopped apple
½ heaping teaspoon cinnamon

Tip

- Prepare the topping just prior to baking the muffins.

1. Preheat oven to 400° F (200° C). Prepare pan(s).
2. Mix cereal, whole wheat pastry flour, all-purpose flour, sugar, baking soda and sea salt together in a medium-size mixing bowl. Set aside.
3. Measure the buttermilk and oil into a large measuring cup. Stir gently. Crack the egg into the cup and mix slightly with a fork, breaking up the yolk.
4. Add the wet ingredients to the dry and stir with a wooden spoon or rubber spatula until well blended. Let the mixture stand for 15 minutes at room temperature. (If you do not cook the muffins right away, cover and refrigerate the batter for up to 2 days.)
5. Prepare the topping. Chop the ¾ cup apple (1 medium apple) and prepare the topping just prior to baking: Mix melted butter, sugar, cinnamon, nuts, and ¼ cup of the chopped apple together in a small bowl. Add ½ cup apple to batter and mix in.
6. Spoon ½ the batter into the bottom of each muffin cup, completely covering the bottoms. Sprinkle ⅔ of the topping evenly over this. Spoon remaining batter over the topping, then remaining topping.
7. Place in oven. Immediately lower the oven temperature to 375° F (190° C). Bake until tester inserted in the center comes out clean (18 minutes), just dry and not pasty.
8. Serve warm or room temperature. May be frozen for up to 1 month.

Yield: 8 standard-size muffins. Preparation time: 20 minutes. Cooking time: 18 minutes. Batter keeps in refrigerator.

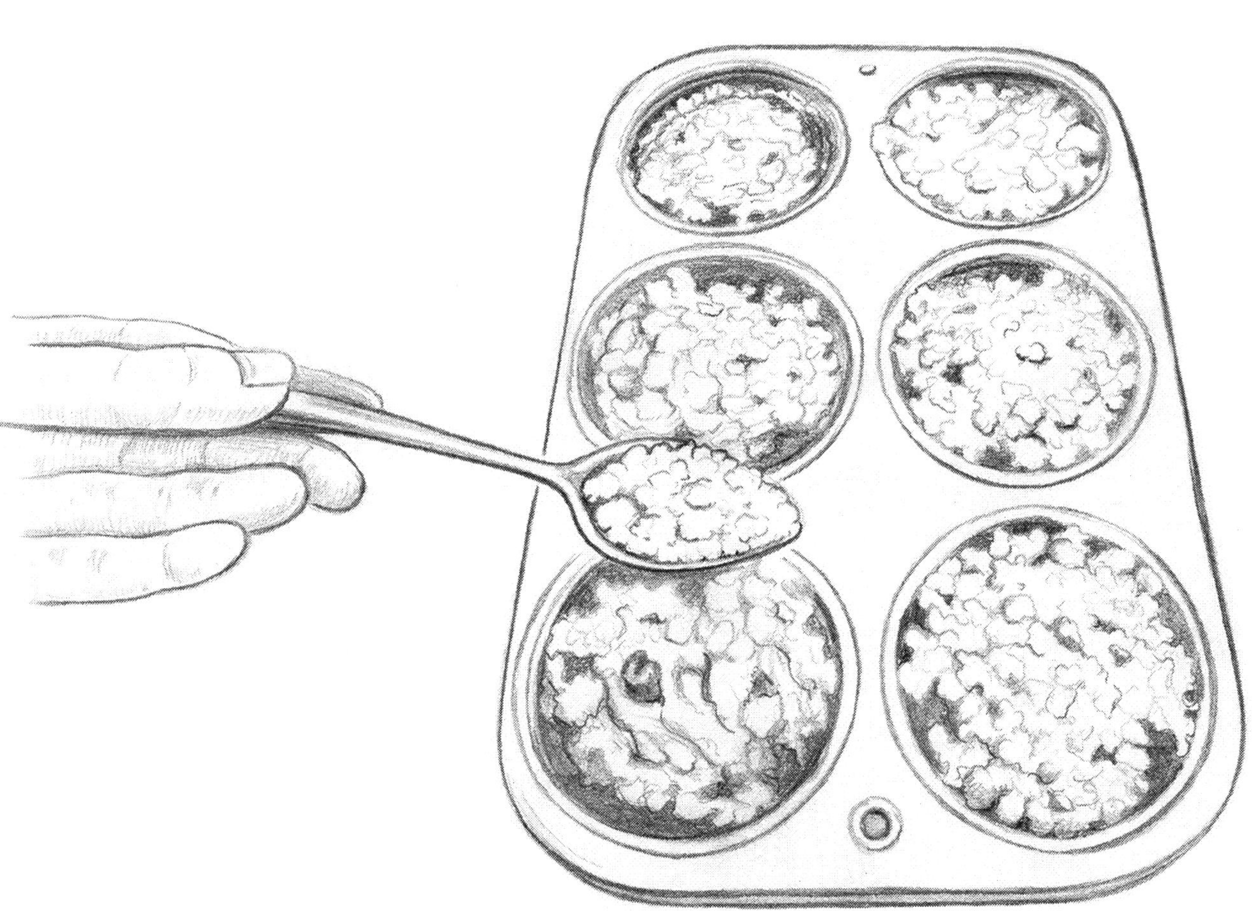

Apple Streusel Nut Bread

NUTS ARE A FLAVOR ENHANCER in many baked items. Happily, most are also good for you. Studies have shown that when eaten as part of a healthy diet, nuts, and especially almonds, help lower cholesterol, substantially reducing the risk of heart disease. For these reasons, I often replace some flour with almond meal in my baking. This recipe is one of my favorite examples.

For the Bread

½ cup whole wheat pastry flour
2 tablespoons mesquite flour
6 tablespoons unbleached all-purpose flour
½ teaspoon baking soda
½ teaspoon baking powder
⅔ cup ground almonds (almond meal)
1 teaspoon cinnamon
1 teaspoon nutmeg
Dash each of cardamom, coriander, and cloves
8 tablespoons (¼ pound) unsalted butter, room temperature
9 tablespoons white sugar (a little of this may be packed light brown sugar)
2 extra-large eggs
2 teaspoons pure vanilla extract
½ cup sour cream
2 large apples (cored, roughly peeled, and thinly-sliced)

Pecan Spice Topping

⅔ cup unbleached all-purpose flour
⅓ cup packed light brown sugar
1 heaping teaspoon cinnamon
3 tablespoons unsalted cold butter (cut up into 3 pieces)
⅔ cup chopped pecans

1. Preheat oven to 350° F (180° C). Prepare pan(s).

2. Sift flours, baking soda, baking powder, almond meal, and spices together onto parchment or wax paper. Set aside.

3. Put the butter and sugar in a standing mixer bowl. Blend well on medium. Add eggs, one at a time, then vanilla and mix. Scrape down sides of the bowl using a rubber spatula.

4. Add dry ingredients to the bowl and mix on low until just incorporated.

5. Add sour cream and mix again on low until just blended.

6. Cut apples into thin slices. Set aside.

7. Prepare topping. In a medium-size bowl, mix the flour, light brown sugar, and cinnamon. Add 1 tablespoon water and the butter. Cut with a pastry cutter or 2 knives held together, until crumbly. Add pecans and mix with a spoon.

8. Scoop ½ of the batter into the pan(s) and lightly press the apples on top of the batter. Then cover the apples with the rest of the batter. (The batter has the tendency to slip off the apples, so use your fingers to keep the batter on.) Sprinkle the topping evenly over the batter. Bake until the tester inserted in the center comes out clean (just dry, not wet) (25-30 minutes for mini-loaves, 35-40 minutes for a 9 x 5-inch loaf). Cool on a rack for at least 20 minutes. To remove, loosen the bread from the pan by running a butter knife gently around the edges. Place the cooling rack on top of the pan. Hold the pan and rack together and turn both over. Place the cooling rack on the counter and lift the pan off the bread. Turn the bread right side up and place on rack to cool completely.

9. Serve the bread warm or room temperature. If wrapped well and refrigerated it will keep for up to 3 days, and if frozen 2 months.

Yield: 1, 9 x 5-inch loaf or 3 mini-loaves. Preparation time: 40 minutes. Cooking time varies.

Variations & Tips

- Try combining apple varieties: the tartness and firmness of Granny Smith works well with the sweet rich flavors of both the Braeburn and the Honeycrisp apples.
- Substitute light sour cream or plain yogurt (preferably a thickly-textured version, like Greek yogurt).
- If you do not have mesquite flour, replace it with 2 tablespoons unbleached all-purpose flour.
- Topping can be made in advance, and stored in a labeled plastic bag in the refrigerator or freezer.

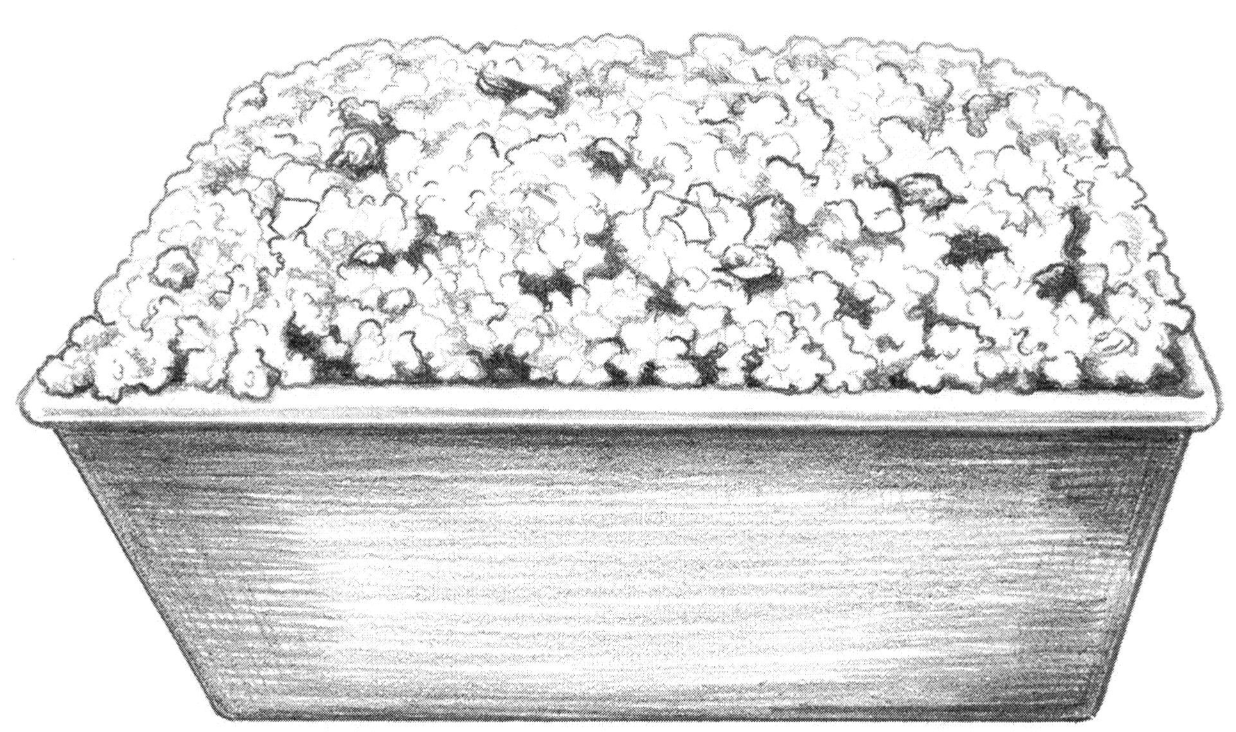

Apple Stir Fry

APPLES PAN-FRIED IN CALVADOS is a delicious alternative to raw apples in muffins and bread. Calvados is an apple brandy made in the Normandy region of France. It is distilled from dry cider with special apple varieties, then aged in French oak barrels before it is blended and bottled. Calvados is also delicious over ice cream, in a mixed drink, or just for sipping. It is available in many liquor stores.

For the Apples

2 tablespoons unsalted butter
2 small-medium size apples
1 tablespoon white or brown sugar
1 tablespoon plus 1-½ teaspoons Calvados

1. Cut peeled or unpeeled apples into small pieces. (Size and shape do not matter.)
2. Melt 2 tablespoons unsalted butter in a medium-large size frying pan. Add the apples and cook, stirring with a wood spoon, over medium-to-high temperature for 5-7 minutes or until brown.
3. Remove the pan from the heat. Stir in the sugar and Calvados, and set aside to cool.
4. Gently stir the apples into the batter, as a last step in a recipe – the same point at which you would add any fruit.

Variations & Tips

- Substitutes for Calvados include pear brandy, equal parts apple juice concentrate and cognac, or apple cider.
- Use apples with a good sweet-tart balance and flesh that does not break down when cooked (such as Granny Smith, Braeburn, and Honeycrisp).
- This quantity is enough for any one of my recipes. When using it, omit 1 tablespoon sugar from the batter recipe.
- When apples are cooked without peeling, they retain their shape and moisture more than if they were peeled. However, if you prefer not to taste the skin, peel the apples.

Yield: enough for 1 bread or muffin recipe. Preparation time: 10 minutes. Cooking time: 5-7 minutes.

Apricot Pecan Oatmeal Bread

APRICOTS ARE AN EXCELLENT source of vitamin A and a very good source of vitamin C and potassium. Apricots and rolled oats are nutritious and a good source of dietary fiber. This dense, chewy bread is a wonderful way to start the day. It needs no embellishments other than a cup of coffee or tea. I adapted my version of apricot bread from one served at a bed and breakfast in St. Paul, Minnesota.

For the Bread

1 cup dried apricots
¾ cup white sugar
1 cup old-fashioned (not quick) rolled oats
¾ cup whole wheat pastry flour
¼ cup unbleached all-purpose flour
2 teaspoons baking powder
½ teaspoon sea salt
½ teaspoon baking soda
1 teaspoon cinnamon
½ cup orange juice
1 large egg
2 tablespoons vegetable oil
1 cup chopped pecans

Variations & Tips

- Walnuts may be substituted for pecans.
- For more even cooking, smooth the batter in the loaf pans from center, so that the sides are higher than the middle.
- Apricots should be organic or free of sulfites.

1. Preheat oven to 350° F (180° C). Prepare pan(s).

2. Chop apricots and place them in a small-to-medium size saucepan and add just enough water to cover. Simmer on a medium-high heat until the apricots are plump and water is absorbed—about 15 minutes. Drain and set them aside to cool.

3. Combine the sugar, rolled oats, whole wheat and all-purpose flours, baking powder, sea salt, baking soda and cinnamon in a large bowl.

4. Place the orange juice, oil and egg in a measuring cup and mix slightly with a fork. Add this to the dry ingredients and stir with a rubber spatula or a large wood spoon. Gently fold the apricots and pecans into the batter and stir just until all the ingredients are incorporated.

5. Scoop the batter into the prepared pan(s) ⅔ full and smooth surface with an offset spatula. Bake until a tester inserted in the center comes out clean (60-65 minutes for the 9 x 5-inch loaf; 45 minutes for the mini-loaves; 20 minutes for miniatures). Tester should come out dry, not pasty.

6. Serve warm or room temperature. This bread tastes great the day it is made and, when well-wrapped, ages nicely, at room temperature for about 3 days. It will keep for a few more days refrigerated and, if frozen, 2 months.

Yield: 1, 9 x 5-inch loaf, 3 mini-loaves, or 36 miniature muffins. Preparation time: 40 minutes. Cooking time varies.

Banana Apricot Bread

THIS WHOLESOME QUICK BREAD is a perfect cross between cake and bread. It has a touch of sweetness, a pleasant dense texture and subtle flavors of banana and apricot that meld together beautifully. For best flavor, use very ripe bananas. When they darken their sugars become concentrated and they become very sweet, just right for baking. A banana is the optimal ripeness for baking just before it turns black. However, black ones are safe to eat.

For the Bread

1 cup whole wheat pastry flour
1 cup unbleached all-purpose flour
¼ cup toasted (or raw) wheat germ
1 teaspoon baking soda
½ teaspoon salt
1 teaspoon cinnamon
Freshly-grated orange zest from 1 orange
½ cup chopped dried apricots
10 tablespoons unsalted butter, room temperature
2 large eggs, room temperature
½ cup packed light brown sugar
1 tablespoon white sugar
½ rounded cup sour cream or Greek yogurt
1-½ cups (approximately 3 large) puréed ripe bananas
1 teaspoon pure vanilla extract
¾ cup chopped walnuts or pecans (optional)

Variations & Tips

- Try using dried tart cherries instead of apricots.
- Use sour cream for a more moist texture.
- Zest is the outer colored part of the peel of citrus fruit. The zest of oranges and lemons are a flavorful addition to many recipes. Zest added to dry flour imparts full flavors.
- The flavors of this bread improve the day after it is baked.

1. Preheat oven to 350° F (180° C). Prepare pan(s).

2. In a large bowl, combine the first 6 ingredients: whole wheat and all-purpose flours, wheat germ, baking soda, salt, and cinnamon. Grate the zest of 1 orange. Chop the dried apricots. Add both to the dry ingredients, stir with a spoon, and set aside.

3. In the bowl of a standing mixer, cream the butter at medium speed. Gradually add the sugar and continue to blend for up to a minute until light and airy. Scrape down the sides of the bowl. With a rubber spatula, beat in the eggs, one at a time, followed by sour cream, bananas, and vanilla extract.

4. Gradually add the flour mixture to the wet ingredients. Mix until dry ingredients are moistened.

5. Turn the batter into the pans and smooth the tops. Bake until tester inserted in the center comes out dry (28-32 minutes for mini-loaves and 15 minutes for miniatures). Cool on a wire rack for 20 minutes. If wrapped well and refrigerated, this will keep for up to 3 days, and, if frozen, 2 months.

Yield: 3 mini-loaves or 36 miniature muffins. Preparation time: 20 minutes. Cooking time varies.

Basic Banana Bread

FRESHLY-BAKED BANANA BREAD is a sweet, comforting, healthy treat, and a good way to use up uneaten ripe bananas before they rot. Banana bread tastes best when made with very ripe bananas, soft and heavily-speckled with brown. There are a few tricks for speeding up ripening. This is my favorite: place bananas in a paper bag with an unpeeled, uncut apple or tomato; leave the paper bag in a warm, dry area; check the bag daily; when the bananas ripen, remove them from the bag. If you cannot wait this long, try another one of my recipes while they ripen. Buttermilk (the slightly sour liquid remaining from churned butter) is another excellent ingredient for moist, light banana bread. Buttermilk resembles whole milk with little or none of the fat. Although it is widely available, I often make it myself by combining distilled white vinegar with milk. That way, I do not have to throw out a partially-used container of buttermilk when it spoils. There are so many good banana breads, but after much experimentation, I've made this my recipe of choice. It is simple and embraces all sorts of variations.

For the Bread

1 cup unbleached all-purpose flour
1 cup whole wheat pastry flour
1 teaspoon baking soda
½ teaspoon sea salt
1 cup (approximately 3) very ripe mashed bananas
⅓ cup plus 1 teaspoon buttermilk
½ cup unsalted butter, room temperature
5 tablespoons white sugar
6 tablespoons packed light brown sugar
2 medium-large eggs, room temperature
1 cup blueberries or ¾ cup coarsely-chopped, semisweet chocolate bar or chips (optional)
⅓ cup chopped walnuts, pecans or unsalted, dry roasted peanuts (optional)

1. Preheat oven to 350° F (180° C). Prepare pan(s).

2. Sift the flours, soda and sea salt onto a sheet of wax or parchment paper. Set aside.

3. Mash bananas in a large transparent measuring cup. Add buttermilk, stir briefly, and set aside.

4. Put the butter and sugar in a standing mixer bowl. Blend well on medium speed. Then scrape down the sides of the bowl with a rubber spatula. Continue mixing for 30 seconds, while adding the eggs, one at a time.

5. Beginning and ending with dry ingredients, add the flour mixture in thirds, alternately with banana/buttermilk. Mix on low after each addition until just combined. Scrape down the sides of the bowl and give a few stirs with the rubber spatula to make sure the batter is blended.

6. Optional: If using blueberries, rinse, dry, and lightly dust with one teaspoon of all-purpose flour just before gently stirring them into the batter with a rubber spatula. If using chocolate and/or nuts, gently stir into the batter. Cook just until a tester comes out dry when inserted in the center (28-32 minutes for mini-loaves and jumbo muffins; 18-21 minutes for standard-size muffins; 15 minutes for miniatures). Cool on a wire rack for 20 minutes. Serve warm or room temperature. If wrapped well and refrigerated, this will keep for up to 3 days, and, if frozen, up to 2 months.

Yield: 3 mini-loaves, 6 jumbo muffins, 12 standard-size muffins, or 36 miniature muffins.
Preparation time: 20 minutes. Cooking time varies.

Variations & Tips

- Plain banana muffins are delicious, but those with blueberries or nuts, or semisweet chocolate chips or shavings are even better.
- For less banana flavor or if you do not have 1 cup of bananas at hand, substitute up to ½ the banana with unsweetened applesauce.
- Try substituting some all-purpose and whole wheat flours with different dry ingredients: ¼ cup almond meal for ¼ cup all-purpose flour, or ¼ cup almond meal and ¼ cup mesquite flour for ¼ cup all-purpose flour and ¼ cup whole wheat flour.
- Make buttermilk by combining 1 tablespoon white vinegar or fresh-squeezed lemon juice with enough of any type of milk to equal 1 cup. Let stand for 5 minutes, until milk begins to curdle.
- If you want to substitute buttermilk for milk in a recipe, it is necessary to alter the amount of baking soda and/or baking powder. Because of the higher acid content in buttermilk, use less baking soda or baking powder. For each cup of buttermilk substituted for milk, use 2 teaspoons less baking powder and ½ teaspoon more baking soda.
- Sifting flour lightens this bread, but is not necessary.
- Do not mix the batter too much, or the bread will be too dense and stiff.

Biscotti with Cranberries, Orange, Nuts, and Semisweet Chocolate

BISCOTTI WITH COFFEE OR TEA are a nice way to start the day. This recipe is a fusion of my many efforts to make perfect biscotti. They are easy to make and especially rewarding for those cooks who enjoy a tactile experience. They are nutritious, yet slightly decadent, with a texture that is not too hard and not too soft – just right. They are well worth making if you are going to be inside for a few hours. When you are done, you have 40 cookies that will keep stored in an airtight container for weeks or frozen for 6 months.

For the Biscotti

⅓ cup dried, coarsely chopped cranberries or cherries (sulfite and sugar-free, if available)
4 teaspoons Grand Marnier or other orange flavored liqueur (You may substitute these with pure orange oil or pure vanilla extract.)
3-½ ounce bar semisweet, high-quality chocolate (50-71% cocoa, depending upon your taste), coarsely chopped
1 cup dry-roasted unsalted nuts, almonds and/or pistachios, coarsely chopped
½ cup (¼ pound) unsalted butter, room temperature
¾ cup white sugar (less 1 tablespoon)
2 large eggs
Zest of a lemon
Zest of an orange
1-½ cups unbleached all-purpose flour
½ cup plus 2 tablespoons whole wheat pastry flour
Large dash cinnamon
1-½ teaspoons baking powder
¾ teaspoon sea salt
1 egg white for egg wash

Variations & Tips

- Use any type of nuts you want. I sometimes substitute walnuts and hazelnuts.
- Try substituting tangerine zest for orange.
- Increase or subtract amounts of berries, chocolate and nuts to suit your taste.
- If you have trouble finding pure orange oil, substitute orange extract or vanilla extract.
- To dry roast raw nuts, bake at 325° F (160° C) for 10 minutes and cool.
- To refresh biscotti, bake in an oven, preheated to 325° F (160° C) for 5 minutes.

1. Preheat oven to 325° F (160° C). Line the baking sheet with parchment.
2. Coarsely chop dried fruit, then put it in a small bowl and soak with the extract or liqueur. Chop chocolate and nuts. Set all aside.
3. Cream butter in the bowl of a standing mixer until light and creamy, about 2 minutes. Scrape down the sides with a rubber spatula.

Yield: 40 cookies. Preparation time: 40 minutes. Cooking time: 35 minutes.

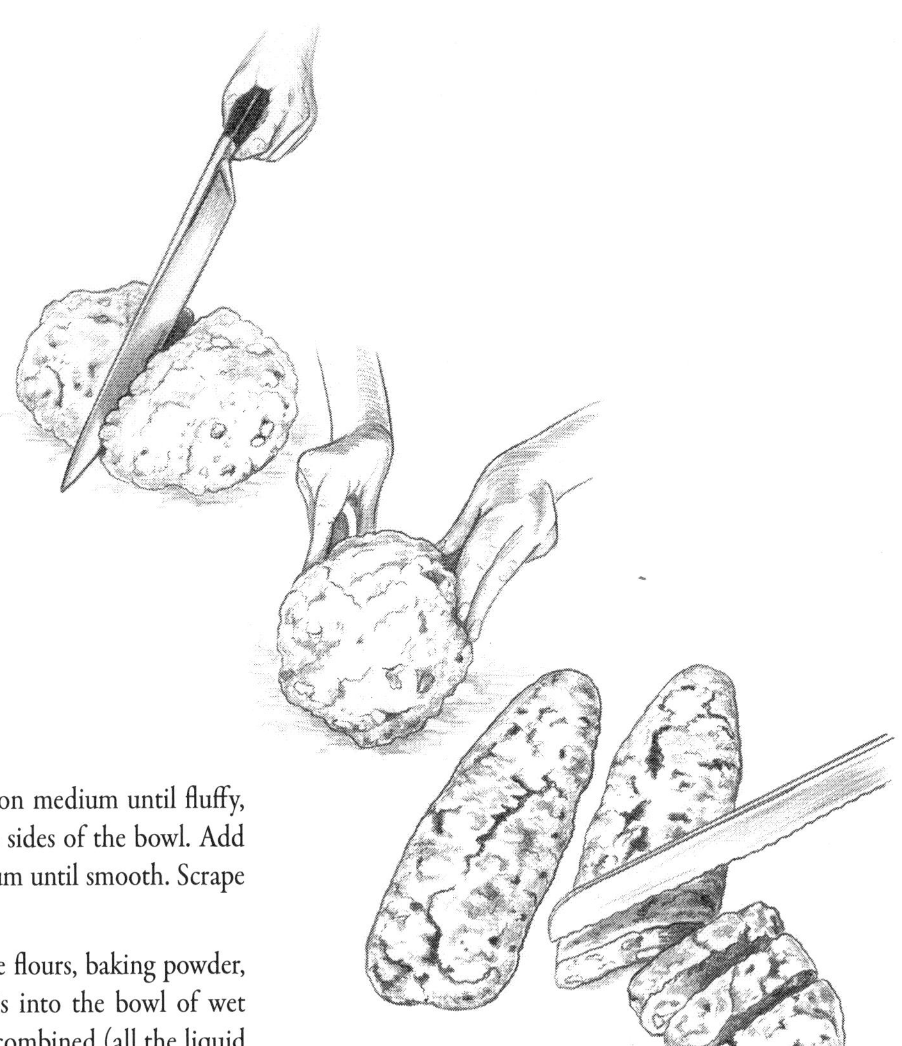

4. Slowly add the sugar and beat on medium until fluffy, about 2 minutes. Scrape down the sides of the bowl. Add 2 eggs and zests and beat on medium until smooth. Scrape down the sides.

5. In a medium-size bowl, mix the flours, baking powder, cinnamon and sea salt. Spoon this into the bowl of wet ingredients. Mix on low until just combined (all the liquid is absorbed and the dry ingredients have been completely incorporated). Add the extract, fruit, nuts and chocolate to the batter and stir with a rubber spatula or large wood spoon. The batter will be very thick.

6. Empty the dough onto a lightly-floured work surface. Cover your hands with flour and kneed and squeeze the dough into a stiff mass. Next, use a long, sharp knife to divide the dough into 2 equal portions. Shape each portion into a log about 12-14 inches long and 2 inches in diameter, pushing in the ends to keep them neat. Gently lift both logs onto the parchment-lined baking sheet, spaced 2 inches apart. Press the top of each log with the heel of your hand to flatten slightly. Whisk the white of the third egg in a small bowl and brush it evenly over each log with a pastry brush. Bake until the logs are set, are light brown, and the tops give slightly when pressed, about 25 minutes.

7. Lift the parchment paper with the rolls onto a wire rack and cool 15 minutes. Transfer logs, one at a time, to a large cutting board. Use a long serrated knife to cut each log on a diagonal into ½-inch wide slices. (Cut slowly, holding your hand against the cut end of the log to minimize crumbling.) Place parchment on 2 cookie sheets. Gently lay the slices on their sides and return the sheets to the oven. Bake until edges are lightly toasted, for 5-9 minutes. Remove pans, turn over each cookie and bake approximately 5 minutes more until light brown. Cool completely on wire racks. Biscotti can be stored in a tin for 1 month or in the freezer for 6.

Brioche à la Bungalow

I WAS INTRODUCED TO THIS RECIPE at the Bungalow, a legendary bar and restaurant that operated for many years in downtown Lexington, Kentucky. Fred made this brioche to accompany John's infamous lunches and brunches. It is wonderful for breakfast, served with jam and butter or just plain. Because it is well-balanced – not too buttery rich – it is also a great complement to lunch or dinner. This recipe does not require much active labor. But it does require "hang around" time. This is the only recipe in my book that uses yeast; however, I feel it is worth the exception.

For the Bread

2-¼ teaspoons (1, ¼-ounce packet) active dry yeast, room temperature
½ cup warm water
2 tablespoons white sugar
2-½ cups unbleached all-purpose flour
½ cup whole wheat pastry flour
1 teaspoon sea salt
¾ cup (1-½ sticks) cold, unsalted butter (keep refrigerated until ready to use)
4 medium-large size eggs, room temperature

1. The brioche cooks at 375° F (190° C); however, because it will not be baked for 3 hours after you begin preparation, do not preheat the oven until step 6. Butter and flour the bottom and bottom corners of a loaf pan.

2. Empty the package of yeast (or crumble the cake) into ½ cup of warm water. Immediately add 2 tablespoons sugar. Stir until dissolved and lump free, and set aside for approximately 20 minutes. During this time, the mixture will proof (bubble and grow), doubling in volume.

3. Add the flour and teaspoon of salt to the standing mixing bowl and combine with a wood spoon. Using a pastry cutter (or 2 knives held closely together), cut the cold butter into the flour mixture until it resembles coarse meal. Then add the yeast mixture, stirring slightly with a wooden spoon or rubber spatula.

4. Add the eggs to this mixture, one at a time, stirring the dough on a low speed after each addition. Blend well, until all of the lumps smooth out. Pour the batter into the greased bread pan.

5. Let the loaf rise for 2 hours in a warm area. To expedite this process, place the bread in a slightly warm oven. (If you choose this method, be careful NOT to cook the brioche in the oven at this point. It should only rise. To warm the oven, preheat it to 100° F. If this low temperature is unavailable, preheat the oven to the lowest possible temperature, then turn if off to allow it to cool down slightly before placing the loaf on the middle rack for 45-60 minutes. Remove the bread from the oven when it has risen.)

6. Preheat oven to 375° F (190° C). Bake the brioche until the top crust is light brown (30 minutes). Turn the loaf out of the pan and onto a cooling rack as soon as it is removed from the oven. Serve warm or room temperature. Do not freeze or refrigerate. If it is not eaten right away, wrap the rest in plastic and finish the next day.

Yield: 1, 9 X 5-inch loaf. Preparation time: 3 hours. Cooking time: 35 minutes.

Variations & Tips

- The original recipe uses only white flour, which results in a lighter, moister product.
- Two forms of yeast are commercially available: dry and wet. Dry includes active dry and instant yeast. Wet yeast is also known as cake, compressed or fresh yeast. Wet yeast spoils easily and has limited availability. Dry and wet yeasts can be substituted for each other (.75 ounces cake or 2-¼ teaspoons dry).
- Although packages are stamped with a "best if used by date," yeast is very perishable, wet much more so than dry. Therefore, I prefer to use dry. Store unopened dry packs in a cool, dry place, refrigerator, or freezer. Once open, it can be stored, tightly wrapped, 4 months in the refrigerator or 6 months in the freezer. Bring to room temperature for 30-45 minutes prior to using.
- Water for yeast should be warm (not hot) to the touch. If in doubt, use a thermometer registered to 110-115° F (43-46° C).

Buttermilk Biscuits with Shredded Cheese and Herb

BISCUITS MAKE A QUICK, delicious breakfast alone, or served warm as an accompaniment to eggs. My recipe is made with buttermilk, so they are exceptionally tender with a subtle tangy taste. For my wheat-free adaptation, see the Gluten-Free Buttermilk Biscuits recipe.

For the Bread

10 tablespoons cold unsalted butter
¾ cup whole wheat pastry flour
1-½ cups unbleached all-purpose flour
2 teaspoons baking powder
½ teaspoon baking soda
1 teaspoon sea salt
1 cup shredded Parmesan cheese
2 teaspoons chopped fresh rosemary
1 cup cold buttermilk

Variations & Tips

- Substitute any hard cheese and herb for the Parmesan and rosemary. There are infinite possibilities: cheddar, Gruyère, Gouda, thyme and chives.
- Cover the unbaked biscuits (either prior to or after cutting into rounds) with plastic wrap, and refrigerate overnight or freeze for up to 1 month.
- The colder the butter and buttermilk, the flakier the biscuits. The small pieces of butter in the dough contribute to the flakiness.
- The higher the quality of cheese, the better the biscuit. For instance, I always use Parmigiano-Reggiano, because of its dependable outstanding quality. (Italian law mandates that cheese with this name be made in specific districts using a prescribed recipe. Parmesan is not included and is usually made outside Italy.)

1. Position a rack in the middle of the oven. Preheat oven to 425° F (215° C). Line the baking sheet with parchment paper.
2. Cut the butter into ½-inch cubes and chill.
3. Combine the flours, baking powder, baking soda and sea salt in a large bowl. Cut in the cold butter, using a pastry cutter (or 2 knives held together) until the mixture looks like coarse meal. Add Parmesan and rosemary and mix briefly with a fork. Then pour in the cold buttermilk and continue to stir with a fork until the dry ingredients are evenly moist.
4. Lightly flour the counter (or work surface); turn out the dough and pat it, just until it comes together, into a ½ to ¾-inch thick circle. (If the dough is too moist, it will stick.) Sprinkle a few more teaspoons flour onto the surface; reshape the circle as you pat it into the flour.
5. Wrap the dough in wax or plastic wrap and chill for at least 30 minutes prior to or the night before baking. Cut into rounds using a 2-½ inch diameter cookie cutter, glass, or canning jar band. Reassemble the scraps and cut or shape them as well.
6. Place the biscuits 1-inch apart on the baking sheet and cook until golden brown (15 minutes). Serve warm or room temperature. These keep for a few days, and taste best warmed for 5 minutes in a 350° F oven. Do not freeze the baked biscuits. Instead, prior to baking, freeze them in a single layer, wrapped and sealed in a plastic bag for 1 month or in the refrigerator for 24 hours. Bake directly from cooler and add a few minutes to the baking time.

Yield: 20, 2-½ inch round biscuits. Preparation time: 20 minutes. Cooking time: 15 minutes. Dough keeps in refrigerator and freezer.

Carrot Bran Muffins

THIS CARROT BRAN is my take on the traditional Morning Glory muffin. Its moist, soft, yet chewy texture, and aromatic spices makes it irresistible. The batter can be used immediately or kept refrigerated for up to 3 days. These bran muffins are best eaten the day or the day after they are made. Do not refrigerate or freeze.

For the Muffins

1-½ cups plus 2 tablespoons wheat bran
⅔ cup plus 2 tablespoons boiling water
⅔ cup unsweetened applesauce
⅓ cup buttermilk
3 tablespoons canola oil
2 small-medium or 1 large egg
3 tablespoons plus 1-½ teaspoons molasses
Zest (chopped) from one orange
1-½ cups shredded carrots (approximately 4 medium), twice shredded
⅓ cup packed light brown sugar
⅓ cup plus 1 tablespoon white sugar
1 cup unbleached all-purpose flour
1 cup whole wheat pastry flour
2 teaspoons baking soda
1 teaspoon baking powder
2 teaspoons cinnamon
1 teaspoon nutmeg
½ teaspoon sea salt
1 cup raisins

Variations & Tips

- 1 cup fresh blueberries may be substituted for raisins. Rinse, dry, and lightly dust with all-purpose flour just prior to gently stirring into the batter.
- Fill empty muffin cups half full of water. This allows all muffins to rise evenly.
- Try using a 2-ounce (4 tablespoons) or ½-ounce (1 tablespoon) mechanical ice cream scoop for making uniform standard and miniature-size muffins.

1. Preheat oven to 375° F (190° C). Prepare pan(s).
2. Mix all-purpose flour, whole wheat pastry flour, baking soda, baking powder, cinnamon, nutmeg, sea salt, and raisins together in a medium-size bowl. Set aside.
3. Put bran into a standing mixer bowl. Add boiling water and stir. Add the applesauce, buttermilk, oil, eggs, molasses, grated carrots, and zest. Mix on low until incorporated. Scrape down the sides of the bowl. Add brown and white sugars, mix until combined and scrape down again.
4. Add the dry ingredients (with raisins) to the wet. Gently mix with a large rubber spatula. Scrape the sides and bottom of the bowl to make sure all of the flour has been absorbed. Mix on low for 10 seconds.
5. Scoop batter directly into muffin pans until each is no more than ⅔ full. Bake until the tester inserted in the center comes out clean, just dry and not pasty (25-30 minutes for jumbo; 21-25 minutes for standard-size; 15 minutes for miniatures).
6. Serve warm or room temperature.

Yield: 6 jumbo, 10 standard-size, or 36 miniature muffins. Preparation time: 45 minutes. Cooking time varies. Batter keeps in refrigerator.

Cappuccino Honey Chip Muffins

RECIPES FOR CAPPUCCINO MUFFINS are commonplace, but mine embraces the best qualities of any I have eaten — light-textured, cinnamon-flavored with a crumb topping. A great way to start the day, accompanied by a cup of coffee or tea.

For the Topping and the Muffins

⅔ cup (10 tablespoons) cold, unsalted butter
½ cup white sugar
1-¼ cups unbleached all-purpose flour
1-½ teaspoons cinnamon
⅓ cup chopped pecans (optional)
1 cup whole wheat pastry flour
2 teaspoons baking powder
½ teaspoon baking soda
½ teaspoon sea salt
2 level tablespoons instant espresso
½ cup honey
2 eggs
¾ cup buttermilk
¾ cup semisweet chocolate chips

Variation

- In place of chips, I often use 7, ½-ounce squares of good-quality, chopped semisweet chocolate (56-71% cocoa).

1. Preheat oven to 375° F (190° C). Prepare pan(s).

2. Put butter and sugar in a standing mixer bowl. Blend well on medium speed. Scrape down sides of bowl with a rubber spatula. Add 1 cup all-purpose flour and 1 teaspoon cinnamon. Blend with mixer just until it resembles crumbs.

3. Prepare topping. Remove ½ cup batter from the standing mixer bowl, and place in small bowl. Break these reserved crumbs between fingers until they resemble coarse crumbs. Mix in chopped pecans. Set aside.

4. To remaining batter, add baking powder, baking soda, sea salt, espresso, honey and eggs. Beat on medium until smooth. Scrape down the sides of the bowl with a rubber spatula.

5. Beginning and ending with dry ingredients, add remaining flour and buttermilk to the batter, alternately, ⅓ at a time. Mix on low after each addition until just blended. Scrape down the sides of the bowl and stir with a rubber spatula until uniformly blended. Add chocolate chips to the batter and stir gently.

6. Pour batter into the prepared pan(s) ⅔ full. Sprinkle the topping evenly over the batter. Bake until a tester inserted in the center comes out clean (30-40 minutes for cake, 25 minutes for jumbo muffins, 15 minutes for standard-size, 10 minutes for miniatures).

7. Serve warm or room temperature. If wrapped well, this keeps up to 3 days, and, if frozen, 2 months.

Yield: 1, 8-10 inch coffee cake; or 6 jumbo, 12 standard-size, or 36 miniature muffins.
Preparation time: 30 minutes. Cooking time varies.

Chuck's Chocolate Chip Peanut Butter Oatmeal Cookies

THIS IS MY FIRST original recipe. I began making it in my early twenties. Since then, there is almost always a tin of these freshly made, delicious cookies in my house. Whenever my dear friend, Chuck, visited from San Francisco, he would "raid the cookie jar." By the time we all got up for breakfast, what had been a full tin eight hours before was now empty. Then, I would bake more for his breakfast from the batter I kept in the refrigerator. Although it might not fit the parameters of this book, I have included this recipe for two reasons. The first is that Chuck would not hesitate to categorize these cookies as breakfast food, and the second is that this has been such a crowd pleaser for so long that I would be remiss in not sharing it.

For the Cookies

1 cup plus 2 tablespoons unbleached all-purpose flour
½ teaspoon baking soda
½ teaspoon sea salt
¼ pound (½ cup) unsalted butter, room temperature
¾ cup combined packed dark brown and white sugar (half of each)
½ teaspoon pure vanilla extract
1 egg
½ cup creamy, unsalted, unsweetened peanut butter
¾ cup old fashioned (not quick) rolled oats
⅔ cup semisweet chocolate chips (more or less to taste)
½ cup chopped nuts (pecans and walnuts)

1. Preheat oven to 375° F (190° C). Prepare pan.

2. Combine the flour, baking soda and sea salt in a small bowl. Set aside.

3. Put the butter and sugars in a standing mixer bowl and cream on high for 15 seconds. Scrape down the bowl with a rubber spatula. Add the vanilla and egg, and beat for a few seconds on medium until incorporated.

4. Add the flour mixture to the wet ingredients. Mix on low speed for 1 minute, followed by a high speed for 1-½ minutes.

5. Scrape down the batter with a rubber spatula.

6. Add the rolled oats and peanut butter to the batter and continue to mix at a high speed for 30 seconds more. Add the chocolate chips and nuts and stir to combine.

7. Scoop large, rounded tablespoons of batter onto the baking sheet, spacing them 1-inch apart. Bake until light brown, but not wet in the middle (which you can see on the top center of the cookie). Cool on the sheet atop a cooling rack for ten minutes. (The cookies will break if handled when hot.) Using a cooking spatula, remove the cookies and let them cool on a cooling rack. Enjoy warm or cooled.

Yield: 20 cookies. Preparation time: 20 minutes. Cooking time: 10-12 minutes. Batter keeps in refrigerator.

Variations & Tips

- Substitute other favorite nuts.
- If you do not want to use peanut butter, omit it. Keep the rest of the recipe the same or substitute the peanut with almond butter.
- These cookies will not stick to the pan, so there is no need to grease the cookie sheet. However, if you like to keep the sheet clean, line the bottom with parchment paper.
- If you do not want to bake the entire batch at once, keep the batter in the refrigerator for up to 4 weeks. To cook, remove the batter from the cooler about an hour prior to baking. (The colder the batter, the longer it takes to cook; cooking less time results in a softer, more desirable finished product.)
- Cookies are light brown when they are done. Because the peanut butter keeps the cookie from browning prematurely, err on the side of under rather than overdone. If they are too dark, they will be hard, rather than soft.
- These cookies keep well for a few days in an airtight container.

Cornbread Mélange

THE MIXTURE OF GRAINS (cornmeal, corn flour, whole wheat pastry flour, and unbleached all-purpose flour) and the buttermilk make this a uniquely crunchy, complex, rich-tasting cornbread. It is a great "fallback" recipe because it's simple, made from ingredients I always have in my kitchen, versatile and popular. Although cornbread is often accompanied with jam and butter, this version stands on its own.

For the Bread

½ cup stone-ground cornmeal
½ cup stone-ground corn flour
⅓ cup whole wheat pastry flour
⅔ cup unbleached all-purpose flour
2-½ teaspoons baking powder
¼ teaspoon sea salt
⅓ cup white sugar
1 cup buttermilk
5 tablespoons unsalted butter, melted
1 large egg

1. Preheat oven to 400° F (200° C). Butter and lightly flour a brownie pan.

2. Mix the dry ingredients together in a large bowl. With a rubber spatula, stir in the buttermilk, butter and egg, and mix until the ingredients are blended and there are no lumps.

3. Pour the batter into the pan, and bake just until a tester inserted in the center comes out dry.

4. Serve warm or at room temperature. The cornbread retains its moist texture and buttery flavor when wrapped well in plastic and stored at room temperature for up to 2 days. Do not freeze.

Variations & Tips

- Add 1 cup lightly-floured blueberries or raspberries.
- Great as an ingredient in a turkey stuffing (or dressing), without fruit.
- Brownie pans are not all the same dimensions. Mine is 8 x 8 inches. If yours is different, adjust the baking time.

Yield: 1, 8 x 8-inch square or 10 standard-size muffins. Preparation time: 15 minutes. Cooking time: 18-20 minutes.

Cranberry Orange Nut Bread

THIS IS A FAVORITE RECIPE. The tartness of the fresh cranberries is offset perfectly by the addition of orange juice and honey. The mix of whole grains results in a cake you can linger over with coffee or tea. This bread tastes better the second day and freezes well. Baked in three mini-loaf pans, it is an ideal winter holiday gift.

For the Bread

1-½ -2 cups fresh cranberries
⅔ cup raisins
1 tablespoon finely grated orange zest
1-¼ cups orange juice, freshly squeezed, if possible
¼ cup plus one tablespoon honey
¼ cup (½ stick or 2 ounces) unsalted butter
½ cup unbleached all-purpose flour
1-½ cups whole wheat pastry or whole wheat bread flour
½ cup wheat germ
½ cup coarsely-chopped walnuts
2-½ teaspoons baking powder
½ teaspoon baking soda
½ teaspoon sea salt

Variations & Tips

- Substitute tangerine for orange juice for a more tart bread.
- Use one 12-ounce bag of cranberries for a double recipe.
- Because of the seasonal nature of cranberries, I used to consider this a fall recipe. No longer. Frozen, unsweetened cranberries are now available year-round. Frozen fruit should not be defrosted prior to using in a recipe. (Dried cranberries lack the same fresh taste and are usually processed with sugar, changing the recipe.)
- It can be tricky to test this bread. Bake until the tester inserted in the center comes out clean, not at all tacky. Bread should not be gummy to the touch—better to overcook than undercook.

1. Preheat oven to 375° F (190° C). Prepare pan(s).

2. Rinse cranberries in a colander. Pat dry and discard very soft and white berries.

3. Place the cranberries and raisins in the bowl of a food processor. Pulse briefly until the berries are roughly cut, then empty into a large pot, along with the orange zest.

4. Add the juice and honey to the pot.

5. Bring the contents to a boil over medium heat. As soon as it comes to a boil, add the butter and stir. Immediately remove the pot from the heat, place it on a cooling rack, and set aside for 30–45 minutes, or until cool.

6. Mix together flours, baking powder, baking soda, sea salt, wheat germ, and nuts in a large bowl. Add to the cooled wet mixture and stir with a rubber spatula or wood spoon until just blended.

7. Spoon the batter into the prepared pan(s) ⅔ full. Bake until the tester inserted in the center comes out clean, not at all gummy (45–55 minutes for the bread pan*; 35 minutes for the mini-loaf pans; 15 minutes for miniatures). Serve at room temperature. If wrapped well and refrigerated, this will keep for up to 5 days, and if frozen, 2 months.

*The top of the bread will be very brown. This is fine.

Yield: 1, 9 x 5-inch loaf, 3 mini-loaves, or 36 miniature muffins. Preparation time: 1 hour. Cooking time varies.

Fruit Purée Breads: Pear, Peach, and Banana

QUICK BREADS WITH PURÉED FRUIT are a delicious way to start the day. By the time I came up with "the" perfect one, I had created three delectable recipes: pear, peach, and banana. They are all variations on the same theme. I use Bosc, D'Anjou, Bartlett, and Comice pears because they are easy to find and work well in baking.

Pear Crunch Bread

For the Bread

1-⅓ cups puréed pears (3 large ripe pears, peeled, cored and puréed in food processor)
⅓ cup plus 2 tablespoons honey
1 teaspoon baking soda
2 teaspoons baking powder
1 cup whole wheat pastry flour
½ cup unbleached all-purpose flour
½ cup almond meal
¼ teaspoon sea salt
1 teaspoon cinnamon
½ teaspoon nutmeg
6 tablespoons unsalted butter, room temperature
¼ cup packed light brown sugar
2 eggs
1 teaspoon pure vanilla extract
1 tablespoon pear liqueur (optional)
¾ cup fresh blueberries or fresh or frozen (sugar-free) diced peaches (optional)

Oatmeal Crunch Topping

2 tablespoons unsalted butter
2 tablespoons packed light brown sugar
½ teaspoon cinnamon
½ cup old-fashioned rolled oats

Peach Nut Bread

For the Peach Nut Bread, follow the Pear Crunch Bread recipe but add one teaspoon cardamom to the dry ingredients and substitute 1-⅓ cups peeled, puréed peaches (3 or 4 large, ripe peaches) for the pears plus peach liqueur or pure vanilla extract. For variety, instead of using the Oatmeal Crunch topping, substitute the Streusel Cinnamon.

Banana Nut Bread

For the Banana Nut Bread, follow the Pear Crunch recipe but substitute 1-⅓ cups puréed bananas (3 large, ripe bananas) for the pears, and omit the pear liqueur. Use a streusel topping. For chocolate lovers, omit the blueberries; instead, add ½ cup semisweet chocolate chips or chopped chunks.

Streusel Cinnamon Topping

3 tablespoons cold unsalted butter
2 tablespoons light brown sugar
2 tablespoons white sugar
1 teaspoon cinnamon
6 tablespoons unbleached all-purpose flour
½ cup ground nuts (pecans and/or walnuts) (optional)

Prepare the topping. With a pastry cutter, or two knives held together, cut the cold butter with the brown and white sugars until the mixture is crumbly and pea-size. Add the flour and cinnamon, and mix gently with a fork. Optional: Add nuts.

Yield: 1, 8-10-inch coffeecake, 3 mini-loaves, 10 standard-size muffins, or 36 miniature muffins.
Preparation time: 45 minutes. Cooking time varies.

1. Preheat oven to 350° F (180° C). Prepare pan(s).

2. Whisk the whole wheat pastry flour, all-purpose flour, almond meal, baking powder, baking soda, sea salt, cinnamon, and nutmeg together in a medium bowl. Set aside.

3. Purée pears, peaches, or bananas in a food processor or blender. Scrape 1-⅓ cups puréed fruit into a measuring cup. Add the honey and mix with spoon until blended. Set aside.

4. Put the butter in a standing mixer bowl. Cream on medium-high until smooth. Scrape down the sides of the bowl using a rubber spatula. Add the brown sugar and mix on medium until blended. Scrape down sides. Add the eggs, 1 at a time, then extract and liqueur (if using), mixing on medium between each addition for a total of 15 seconds. Scrape down sides.

5. Add the honey/fruit purée to the butter mixture and mix on medium until just combined. Scrape down sides.

6. Add ½ the dry ingredients to the wet and mix gently with a rubber spatula or wood spoon until just combined. Add the remaining dry ingredients and mix again until just combined.

7. Optional: Prepare any non-puréed fruit you add to the batter (wash and dry blueberries; peel and coarsely chop peaches). Place fruit on a large plate. Sprinkle 1 teaspoon all-purpose flour evenly over fruit. Cover fruit with flour by lightly shaking the plate. Gently mix fruit into the batter.

8. Prepare topping. Melt butter. Add brown sugar and cinnamon, and mix. Add ½ cup rolled oats and mix thoroughly.

9. Pour ½ the batter into the pan(s). Sprinkle ½ the topping over the batter. Pour remaining batter over topping and distribute evenly. Sprinkle remaining topping. Bake until tester inserted in the center comes out clean, just dry and not pasty (40-45 minutes for coffeecake; 30-35 minutes for mini-loaves; 18 minutes for standard-size muffins; 12-15 minutes for miniatures).

10. Serve warm or room temperature. If wrapped well and refrigerated, it will keep for up to 3 days, and, if frozen, 6 weeks.

Variations & Tips for All Breads

- For miniature muffins, put the topping on the top of each muffin. It is not necessary to put it in the center.
- Fruit liqueurs impart a subtle essence of the fruit. While a nice addition, it is definitely not crucial. Use pure vanilla extract instead.
- Cardamom and peach is a great combination. The spice draws out the floral notes in peaches.
- Baking pans should be no more than ⅔ full.
- Lightly dust fruit with 1 teaspoon flour just before adding to the batter. This helps the fruit from sinking during baking.
- Frozen, unsweetened peaches may be substituted for fresh.
- Topping can be made in advance and stored in the refrigerator or freezer in a labeled plastic bag.

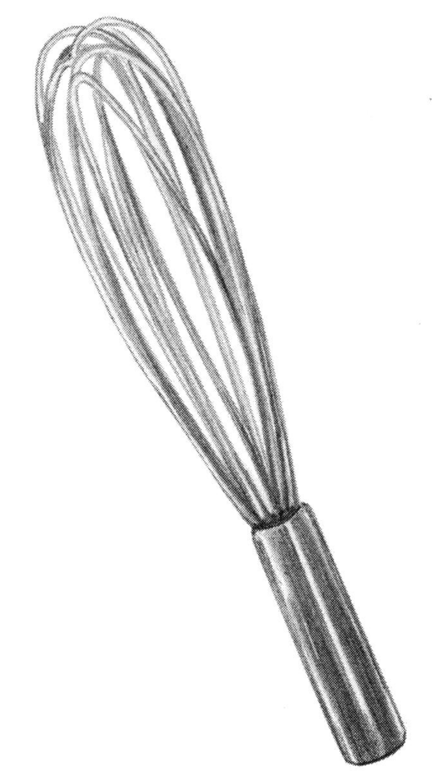

Grated Apple Bread

THIS BREAD EMBODIES THE PERFECT combination of tart to sweet. Although there are plenty of apple bread recipes to choose from, many are too oily, too sugary, too bland, or too moist. I worked on this one until it was just right. An important ingredient is a great baking apple, one that has a good sweet-tart balance and flesh that will not break down with cooking. The sweeter, spicier apples such as Braeburn and Honeycrisp are good choices. Granny Smiths are one of the most popular tart apples and great for baking when combined with sweeter, spicier apples.

For the Bread

4-½ tablespoons unsalted butter
1 teaspoon grated lemon zest
3 tablespoons fresh lemon juice
2 cups (3-4 large) coarsely-packed grated apples
⅓ cup raisins
1 cup unbleached all-purpose flour
1 cup whole wheat pastry flour
2 teaspoons baking powder
½ teaspoon baking soda
¼ teaspoon sea salt
1-½ teaspoons cinnamon
½ cup packed light brown sugar
1 large egg, beaten
¼ teaspoon pure vanilla extract
¼ cup finely-chopped nuts (optional)

Variations & Tips

- Look for regional and heirloom varieties of apples at farmers' markets/specialty grocers.
- Lemons are easier to handle whole, so zest them prior to cutting them open. Use a microplane zester or the side of a manual grater with small holes.
- One lemon will produce about 2 tablespoons juice.

1. Preheat oven to 350° F (180° C). Prepare pan(s).

2. Heat butter on low temperature until it just melts. Place melted butter in the bowl of a standing mixer. Set aside to cool.

3. Peel and chop the zest from 1 lemon. Then squeeze the juice into a cup and remove the seeds. (If there is not enough juice, open another lemon.)

4. Roughly peel apples. Then, coarsely grate them using a food processor or the side of a manual grater with the largest holes. Scoop the apples into a medium bowl. Add the lemon juice and the raisins.

5. Put the all-purpose flour, whole wheat flour, baking powder, baking soda, sea salt, and cinnamon in a medium bowl. Add the lemon zest and nuts, and gently mix with a spoon. Break open the egg into a small cup. Set aside.

6. Add the egg and sugar to the cooled melted butter. Beat slowly for a few seconds until combined. Add apple mixture and vanilla and mix for 30 seconds on medium. Add the dry ingredients. Stir with either a wood spoon or rubber spatula until uniformly combined. Scrape down the sides of the bowl with a rubber spatula.

7. Pour the batter into the pan(s) ⅔ full and smooth the surface of the breads with an offset spatula. Bake until a tester inserted in the center comes out clean (40-45 minutes for the 9 x 5-inch loaf; 30 minutes for the mini-loaves; 25 minutes for the standard-size muffins; 15 minutes for the miniatures).

8. This bread can be served warm or room temperature. If wrapped well and refrigerated, it will keep for up to 3 days, and, if frozen, 3-4 weeks.

Yield: 1, 9 x 5-inch loaf, 3 mini-loaves, 12 standard-size, or 24 miniature muffins.
Preparation time: 40 minutes. Cooking time varies.

Honey Pecan Streusel Coffee Cake

HONEY CAKE IS MADE ALL OVER the world, in many different ways, with a variety of ingredients. The use of oil in many of these traditional recipes makes for a very moist, dense cake. In this recipe, I opted for a less wet texture and used butter in place of oil, in addition to a streusel topping. Like most honey cakes, this is a good keeper and can be made a couple of days ahead.

For the Cake

⅔ cup unsalted butter, room temperature
10 tablespoons packed light brown sugar
1 teaspoon cinnamon
1 cup unbleached all-purpose flour
⅓ cup finely chopped pecans
2 teaspoons baking powder
½ teaspoon baking soda
½ teaspoon sea salt
½ cup plus 2 tablespoons honey
2 eggs
1-¼ cups whole wheat pastry flour
¾ cup buttermilk

Tips

- The flavors of this honey cake improve as it cools.
- If a cracked egg has an unwanted piece of shell, scoop it up with a large piece of an egg shell.

1. Preheat oven to 350° F (180° C). Prepare pan(s).

2. Put butter and 10 tablespoons light brown sugar in a standing mixer bowl. Cream on medium to high speed until they are fully integrated. Add the cinnamon and 1 cup unbleached all-purpose flour, and mix on low, just until the batter resembles a crumbly mixture.

3. Put ½ of this mixture (about 1 cup) in a medium-size bowl to use as a topping. Work this between your fingers until it resembles coarse crumbs. (If the mixture is too soft to crumble, place the bowl in the freezer for 10 minutes, remove, and then crumble.) Stir in chopped pecans. Set aside.

4. To the batter remaining in the standing bowl, add baking powder, baking soda, sea salt, honey, and eggs. Beat until smooth. Add the remaining 1-¼ cups whole wheat pastry flour and buttermilk, in thirds, beginning and ending with dry ingredients. Mix on low just until the flour is absorbed, then set aside.

5. Divide half the batter evenly into the pan(s). Sprinkle ½ the crumb mixture over this. Finish with the rest of the batter and then the remaining crumb topping.

6. Cook just until a tester inserted in the center comes out dry (25 minutes for the mini-loaves and the cake). Cool on a rack for 20 minutes. Serve at room temperature. Wrap well and store outside the refrigerator for up to 2 days and 2 months in the freezer.

Yield: 1, 8-10 inch springform cake or 3 mini-loaves. Preparation time: 40 minutes. Cooking time: 25 minutes.

Maple Syrup Bread

MAPLE SYRUP is one of the many wonders of the world. It takes about 40 gallons of the sweet, runny sap of the sugar maple tree to make just one gallon of syrup. Maple syrup is smooth and silky-textured, with sweet, distinctive caramel-vanilla flavors and beautiful amber color. In addition to being delicious, it is an excellent source of manganese and a good source of zinc.

For the Bread

¾ cup almond meal
¾ cup whole wheat pastry flour
1-½ cups unbleached all-purpose flour
1 tablespoon baking powder
1 teaspoon sea salt
10 tablespoons unsalted butter, room temperature (for 2 or more hours)
2 cups pure maple syrup, room temperature
3 large egg yolks
2 large eggs
1-¼ cups whole milk, room temperature
¾ cup coarsely chopped walnuts

Variations & Tips

- I think that the texture and maple sweetness of this recipe are perfect. But, if you want a less sweet product, reduce the amount of syrup by ¼-½ cup.
- The quality of maple syrup varies in color, taste and consistency. All maple syrups are labeled with a grade, based on official government grading systems. (Canada, producer of 80 percent of the world's maple syrup, and the United States have different grading systems.) Light to medium amber color and Grade A syrups have a mild maple flavor. I prefer to use the dark amber and Grade B syrups for baked goods where the richer and fuller flavors shine through.
- Store unopened container of maple syrup in a cool dry place. It should be kept in the refrigerator once opened. Maple syrup can be frozen, and defrosted prior to use.

1. Preheat oven to 325° F (165° C). Prepare pan(s).
2. Sift almond meal, whole wheat pastry flour, unbleached all-purpose flour, baking powder, and sea salt onto parchment or wax paper. Set aside.
3. Scrape the very soft butter into a standing mixer bowl. Beat on medium-high speed for a few minutes, or until creamy. Scrape down sides with a rubber spatula. Add the maple syrup and beat on medium for 2 minutes or until smooth. Scrape down the sides of the bowl a few times during this process. Note: If the butter is not soft enough, it will not totally blend into the syrup. Instead, specks will remain afloat, which also works but is harder to work with.
4. Add the egg yolks, and then the whole eggs, one at a time, beating on medium after each addition. Then add the flour mixture, a third at a time, alternately with the milk, beginning and ending with the dry ingredients. Mix on low after each addition, until just combined. Scrape down the sides of the bowl to make sure all the flour has been absorbed. Gently stir in the walnuts.
5. Fill each pan ⅔ to ¾ full. Bake until a tester inserted into the center comes out clean (40 minutes for mini-loaves, 25-30 minutes for muffins).
6. Cool in pan on a wire rack for 10 minutes. Run a small knife around the sides of the bread to loosen, then invert onto the racks. Serve warm or at room temperature. Wrapped well, these will keep for up to 3 days at room temperature and 2 months in the freezer.

Yield: 4 mini-loaves or 12 standard-size muffins. Preparation time: 20 minutes. Cooking time varies.

Maple Syrup

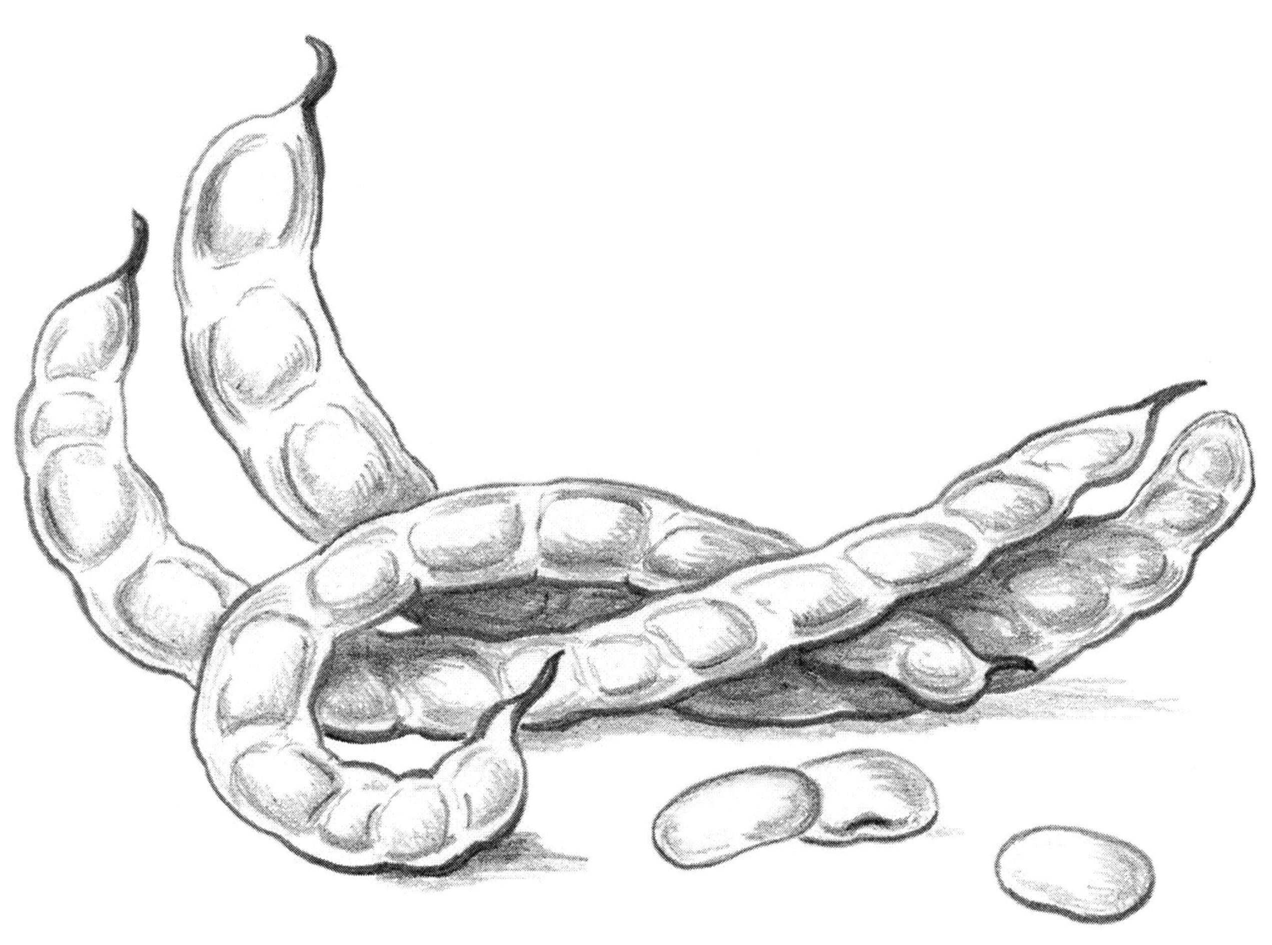

Mesquite Almond Tea Cake

THE FIRST TIME I TASTED a cake made with mesquite flour, I was hooked. Mesquite flour is light beige, gluten-free, nutritious, fragrant, and has a delicate and distinctive flavor—slightly sweet with a mild graham cracker-like flavor, nutty with a hint of molasses. It addition, it is nutritious. The taste is quite strong, though, so I substitute it for only 25% of the total amount of flour used. Mesquite flour, or meal, is made from the pods of mesquite trees growing in the American Southwest and desert climates worldwide. It's definitely worth seeking out, and has become increasingly popular in recent years. Depending upon where you live, it can be found in the baking section of your grocery store, as well as at specialty grocers like Whole Foods, and online (try NativeSeeds.org or flordemayoarts.com). For my wheat-free adaptation, see the Gluten-Free Mesquite Almond Tea Cake recipe.

For the Bread

⅓ cup mesquite meal
⅓ cup almond meal (ground almonds)
¾ cup plus 1 tablespoon and 1 teaspoon whole wheat pastry flour
¼ cup unbleached all-purpose flour
1 teaspoon baking powder
¼ teaspoon sea salt
¼ cup agave nectar and ¼ cup maple syrup
⅓ cup unsalted butter
¾ cup milk (any kind works)
1 large or 2 small eggs
1 teaspoon pure vanilla extract
1 teaspoon pure almond extract

Variations & Tips

- Try sifting the dry ingredients to lighten this dense cake.
- I often use mini-loaf pans for gifts.
- Break eggs into a cup and not directly into the batter. If you need to remove a stray egg shell, it is easier.
- Most mesquite flour is uncooked. If you see the limited roasted variety, try it. Although more expensive than the uncooked, the deep carob taste is worth a splurge.

1. Preheat oven to 350° F (180° C). Prepare pan(s).
2. Melt the butter and cool. Place dry ingredients in a sifter and sift onto parchment or wax paper. Set aside.
3. Place the maple syrup, agave, and milk into a large measuring cup, then add the cooled butter.
4. Break the egg(s) into a small cup and stir slightly with a fork. Add to the wet mixture along with the vanilla and almond extracts and stir slightly. Pour into the bowl of a standing mixer.
5. Add the dry ingredients to the bowl, ¼ at a time, mixing on low until the flour is combined. Using a rubber spatula, scrape the sides of the bowl to make sure all of the flour has been absorbed.
6. Pour or spoon the batter into the prepared pan(s) ⅔ full. Smooth the surface with an offset spatula. Then bake until the tester inserted in the center comes out clean (40–45 minutes for the bread pan; 30 minutes for the mini-loaf pans; 12 minutes for miniatures). Serve warm or room temperature. If wrapped well, it will keep for up to 3 days, and 2 months frozen.

Yield: 1, 9 x 5-inch loaf, 2 mini-loaves, or 36 miniature muffins. Preparation time: 20 minutes. Cooking time varies.

Orange Bread with Agave, Maple Syrup, and Chocolate

MANY YEARS AGO I moved from the East to Arizona, where I discovered a whole new world with a distinct landscape, cultural heritage and food. One is agave nectar, a sweetener made from the agave, the same plant used to produce tequila in Mexico. Over the years, agave nectar has become increasingly mainstream and is now widely available in grocery and specialty stores. Diabetics have embraced it as a nutritious substitute for other sweeteners. The lighter agave nectar is similar in taste to honey; the darker tastes more like maple syrup. Both have the consistency of honey. However, learning how to bake with agave nectar is a bit of an art, as it can change the consistency of baked goods. My orange bread is an outstanding example of how agave nectar can be successful in baking.

For the Bread

7 tablespoons unsalted butter, melted
⅓ cup plus ¼ cup unbleached all-purpose flour
⅓ cup almond meal
¾ cup plus 1 tablespoon and 1 teaspoon whole wheat pastry flour
1 teaspoon baking powder
¼ teaspoon sea salt
1 tablespoon white sugar
1-¾ ounces (5 squares) semisweet chocolate (56-71%) bar, roughly chopped
½ cup coarsely chopped pecans (optional)
¼ cup agave nectar (preferably Blue Agave)
¼ cup maple syrup
¾ cup orange juice, preferably fresh
Grated zest from 2 oranges
2 medium eggs
1 teaspoon pure vanilla extract
1 teaspoon orange extract

1. Preheat oven to 350° F (180° C). Prepare pan(s).

2. Melt the butter and cool. Place dry ingredients in a sifter and sift onto parchment or wax paper. Set aside.

3. Chop the chocolate into pea-size pieces with a knife on a cutting board and set aside. (If using chocolate chips, measure ¼-⅓ cup.) Chop the pecans in the same manner. Set aside.

4. Place the agave, maple syrup, and orange juice into a large measuring cup, then add the cooled, melted butter.

5. Break the eggs into a small cup and stir slightly with a fork. Add them to the wet mixture along with the vanilla and orange extracts, and stir slightly. Pour into the bowl of a standing mixer.

6. Add the dry ingredients and orange zest to the bowl, ¼ at a time, mixing on low until the flour is combined. Using a rubber spatula, scrape the sides of the bowl to make sure all of the flour has been absorbed. Add the chocolate and pecans to the batter. Stir with rubber spatula until incorporated. Batter is thin. This is fine.

7. Pour or spoon the batter into the prepared pans so that they are ⅔ full and smooth the surface with an offset spatula. Bake until the top springs back when lightly touched and a cake tester inserted in the center comes out clean (40 minutes for the mini-loaf pans; 15-20 minutes for the miniatures). Cool on a wire rack for 20 minutes. Cut foil, parchment, or wax paper larger than the rack.

8. Prepare glaze. Stir the orange and lemon juices, and sugar together in a small bowl. Remove the bread from the pan(s) and place on the cooling rack. Put the rack over the cut paper. With a pastry brush, cover the entire warm cake with the glaze. (Note: for a slightly crunchier glaze texture, baste 15 minutes after turning out cake onto rack.) Serve at room temperature. If wrapped well and refrigerated, it will keep for up to 3 days, and, if frozen, 2 months.

Yield: 2 mini-loaves or 36 miniature muffins. Preparation time: 30 minutes. Cooking time varies.

For the Glaze
1 tablespoon fresh-squeezed lemon juice
1 tablespoon fresh-squeezed orange juice
¼ cup white sugar

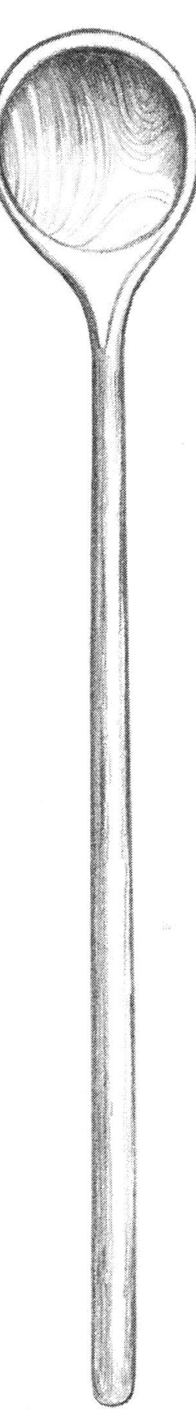

Variations & Tips

- If you want a change, try substituting fine-ground hazelnuts for almond meal.
- Tangerine juice and/or zest may be substituted for orange. However, tangerine is more tart than orange.
- If you are feeling particularly adventurous and have either Grand Marnier or Cointreau liqueur, try substituting it for the orange extract. You can substitute vanilla extract for orange.
- I use chocolate bars for more control over size and quality of the chocolate. However, it is fine to use ⅓-½ cup miniature semisweet chocolate chips instead.
- Because this is a dense cake, I recommend sifting the dry ingredients to lighten it.
- Cooled butter should not solidify. Bring wet ingredients to room temperature prior to adding melted butter to prevent butter from hardening.
- Pure orange extract may be hard to find. It is available at large specialty stores, such as Whole Foods.
- As a rule, I only replace ½ the sugars with agave and in the following proportions: honey, replace with equal amounts agave; maple syrup, replace with equal amounts agave; white sugar, for every one cup sugar, use ⅔ cup agave minus ¼ cup liquid; brown sugar, for every 1 cup sugar, use ⅔ cup agave minus 2 tablespoons liquid.

Peach Oatmeal Muffins

THIS CHEWY, WHOLESOME BREAD is always convenient to make. Because I use dried fruit, it can be made year-round. Dried apricots, cherries, pears, and apples are delicious substitutes.

For the Muffins

1 cup dried peaches
¼ cup tepid water or peach liquor
2-⅓ cups old-fashioned rolled oats
½ cup whole wheat pastry flour
½ cup unbleached all-purpose flour
½ cup packed light brown sugar
¼ cup plus 2 tablespoons white sugar
2 tablespoons oat bran
2 tablespoons wheat germ
2 teaspoons ground cinnamon
1 teaspoon cardamom
1-½ teaspoons baking soda
½ teaspoon sea salt
1 cup buttermilk
⅔ cup unsalted melted butter, cooled
2 large eggs
1 teaspoon pure vanilla extract

Pecan Spice Topping

⅔ cup unbleached all-purpose flour
⅓ cup packed light brown sugar
1 heaping teaspoon cinnamon
3 tablespoons unsalted cold butter (cut into small pieces)
⅔ cup chopped pecans (optional)

Variations & Tips

- If available, use organic, sulfite-free dried fruit.
- Depending upon the fruit you use, you can vary the soaking liquid. Try Calvados or apple juice with apples or pear liqueur or juice with pears.
- I think a topping in baking is often nice, although not always necessary. Use it here if you have the time and/or inclination. Freeze or refrigerate the leftover.
- Do not fill pans more than ⅔.

1. Preheat oven to 375° F (190° C). Prepare pan(s).

2. Soak peaches in warm water (or peach liqueur) for 15 minutes, until all or most of the liquid is absorbed. Pat the fruit dry, then roughly chop. Reserve any liquid.

3. In a large bowl, whisk oats, wheat and all-purpose flours, sugars, oat bran, wheat germ, cinnamon, cardamom, baking soda, and sea salt with a large spoon.

4. Add buttermilk, butter, eggs, and vanilla to dry ingredients. Use a hand whisk or one from a standing mixer just to blend. Stir in any remaining liquid from the soaked fruit. Let stand 5 minutes.

5. Prepare topping. With a pastry cutter (or 2 knives held together), cut the cold butter with the brown and white sugars in a medium bowl until the mixture is crumbly and pea-size. Add the flour and cinnamon. Mix gently with a fork. Optional: Add nuts. Set aside.

6. Fold fruit into the batter. Distribute ½ the batter among prepared pans. Evenly cover with half the topping, then remaining batter, and finally remaining topping. (If not using a topping, you still fill each cup ⅔ full.) Bake until tester inserted into the center comes out clean (24 minutes for mini-loaves; and 28 minutes for jumbo, 20 minutes for standard; and 15 for miniature muffins).

7. Serve warm or room temperature. If wrapped well and refrigerated, will keep for up to 3 days, and, if frozen, 2 months.

Yield: 3 mini-loaves; or 6 jumbo, 9 standard-size, or 24 miniature muffins. Preparation time: 25 minutes. Cooking time varies.

Peanut Butter Chip Muffins

THESE MUFFINS HAVE A SUBTLE peanut butter taste and just the right amount of chocolate. There is nothing sophisticated or gourmet about them. They're just really good. Peanut butter is nutritious and rich in cholesterol-lowering fats but high in calories. So, as with many delicious foods, it should be eaten in moderation. (If allergic to peanuts, substitute almond butter for peanut butter.)

For the Muffins

1-⅓ cups unbleached all-purpose flour
⅔ cup whole wheat pastry flour
2 teaspoons baking powder
¼ teaspoon sea salt
¾ cup coarsely-chopped, semisweet chocolate bar or chips
¾ cup unsalted, creamy or chunky, "all natural," unprocessed peanut butter, room temperature
¾ cup white or packed light brown sugar
1 large egg
1 cup milk (any type)
1 teaspoon pure vanilla extract

Walnut Chocolate Streusel Topping

½ cup white sugar
¼ cup unsweetened cocoa powder
3 tablespoons cold, unsalted butter, cut into small pieces
¼ cup finely chopped walnuts

Variations & Tips

- Try marbleizing the muffins. Using a small sharp knife, lightly draw through the batter in a snaking pattern.
- Buy all-natural peanut butter, which should only have 2-3 ingredients: peanuts, oil, and sometimes salt. I prefer unsalted because it is easier to control salt content in a recipe. Remember, since it's natural, you'll have to mix it well before using.
- Chocolate chips (as well as nuts and dry fruit) are more evenly distributed in the batter if you stir them directly into the dry ingredients.
- These muffins taste best the day after baking.

1. Preheat oven to 350° F (180° C). Prepare pan(s).

2. Sift the all-purpose and whole wheat flours, baking powder, and sea salt into a large bowl. Add the chocolate chunks and stir.

3. Place the peanut butter into the bowl of a standing mixer. Mix on medium speed while gradually adding the sugar, egg, milk, and vanilla extract. Pour into the bowl of dry ingredients and mix with a rubber spatula until just combined.

4. Prepare topping. In medium-size bowl, combine sugar and cocoa. Use a fork to break up any hard pieces of cocoa. Add the butter pieces. With pastry cutter (or 2 knives held together), cut the butter into the sugar/cocoa until it resembles coarse crumbs. Add the walnuts and mix gently with a spoon.

5. Use ½ the batter to fill each muffin cup ⅓ full. Sprinkle ½ the topping equally over these. Spoon the remaining batter on top, and finish with the rest of the streusel.

6. Bake until tester inserted in the middle comes out just moist, but without any uncooked crumbs attached (18-21 minutes for the standard and 13-15 minutes for the miniature muffins). Cool on a wire rack for 20 minutes. Wrapped well, these will keep for up to 3 days at room temperature and 2 months in the freezer.

Yield: 12 standard-size or 24 miniature muffins. Preparation time: 20 minutes. Cooking time varies.

Pear Ginger Bread

GINGER HAS A WARM TASTE with warming properties. It also has important medicinal qualities. This powerful herb has been used as a natural remedy for many ailments for centuries, from the treatment of cancer to migraines. Ginger pairs well with many ingredients. In this bread, the combination of ginger with pear is delicious. Because they are easy to find and work well for baking, I often use Bartlett, Comice, Bosc, or D'Anjou pears. They should be firm to the touch. If too hard, they will not have enough flavor. If too soft, there will be too much liquid.

For the Bread

1-¼ cups whole wheat pastry flour
1-¼ cups unbleached all-purpose flour
2 teaspoons baking powder
1 teaspoon baking soda
1 teaspoon ground ginger
1 teaspoon ground cinnamon
¼ teaspoon ground allspice
½ teaspoon sea salt
½ cup chopped crystallized ginger
¼ pound (½ cup) unsalted butter, room temperature
10 tablespoons packed light or dark brown sugar
2 large eggs
½ cup dark or light molasses
½ cup buttermilk
2 large, firm, ripe pears

Variations & Tips

- Try substituting 1 cup chopped, dry pears for fresh ones. Soak dry pears in warm water for 15 minutes. Drain, pat dry and roughly chop.
- Substitute apples for pears.
- Crystallized or candied ginger is a type of confection in which the root is cooked in sugar until soft. It is available in specialty stores such as Whole Foods and Trader Joe's, plus many others.
- If you have some extra topping hanging around, sprinkle a little on top of this bread.
- Butter and eggs can be brought from refrigerator to room temperature in 20 minutes.

1. Preheat oven to 350° F (180° C). Prepare pan(s).
2. In a medium bowl, whisk together flours, baking powder, baking soda, ground ginger, cinnamon, allspice, sea salt, and crystallized ginger.
3. Put the butter and brown sugar in a standing mixer bowl. Blend well on medium-high. Add eggs, one at a time, beating on medium-low after each addition. Pour in molasses and mix at medium-low before scraping down the sides of the bowl with a rubber spatula.
4. Beginning and ending with dry ingredients, alternately add flour mixture and buttermilk to the bowl and mix on low until just incorporated. Scrape down the sides of the bowl with a rubber spatula, mixing until just blended.
5. Roughly peel and cut pears into small pieces.
6. Mix the pears into the batter and immediately spoon into the prepared pans.
7. Bake until a tester inserted in the center comes out clean (35 minutes for mini-loaves; and 25 minutes for jumbo, and 18 minutes for miniature muffins).
8. Serve at room temperature. Wrapped well and refrigerated, this keeps for up to 3 days, and, if frozen, 2 months.

Yield: 4 mini-loaves; or 8 jumbo or 36 miniature muffins. Preparation time: 30 minutes. Cooking time varies.

Pecan Sour Cream Dream Cake

AT A GLANCE, THIS MIGHT APPEAR to be just another coffee cake. It's not. The lightly rich, delicate flavor and texture of this morning cake is a cross between a coffee cake and a pound cake. Regardless of whether I use low-fat sour cream or full-fat yogurt, it's great. I have been making it for years because it is easy, delicious and fast.

For the Cake

1 cup whole wheat pastry flour
1 cup unbleached all-purpose flour
1 teaspoon baking powder
1 teaspoon baking soda
2 teaspoons cinnamon
1 teaspoon nutmeg
Dash each of cardamom, coriander, and cloves
¾ cup (1-½ sticks or 6 ounces) unsalted butter, room temperature
½ cup white sugar
½ cup packed light brown sugar
2 medium-large eggs
1 teaspoon pure vanilla extract
1 cup (½ pint) full-fat, low-fat sour cream or Greek style yogurt

Simple Pecan Topping

¾ cup chopped pecans
2 tablespoons white sugar
2 tablespoons packed light brown sugar
1 heaping teaspoon ground cinnamon

Variations & Tips

- Although I call this a pecan cake, feel free to substitute walnuts, a combination of both, or any other favorite nut.
- This is equally luscious with either ⅓-½ cup semisweet chocolate chips, or seasonal fruit, such as 1 cup of blueberries and/or raspberries.
- Dust berries with 1-3 teaspoons flour, just prior to adding to batter, to prevent sinking during baking.
- For a lighter cake, I sometimes sift the dry ingredients.
- Greek style yogurt has a thick texture and is good for baking.

1. Preheat oven to 350° F (180° C). Prepare pan(s).
2. Mix together or sift the dry ingredients in a medium-size bowl. Set aside.
3. Prepare the topping. Mix the four ingredients together in a small bowl. Set aside.
4. Put butter and sugar in a standing mixer bowl. Mix on medium speed until sugar and butter are well blended. Scrape down the sides with a rubber spatula. Then, add eggs, one at a time, followed by vanilla and sour cream or yogurt and mix on medium-high until combined. Scrape down sides.
5. Spoon the dry ingredients into the batter, a third at a time, and mix on low, just until the flour is absorbed. Using a rubber spatula, scrape down the sides and stir a few more times. (If adding fruit or chocolate, add to batter and stir gently.)
6. Spoon half the batter into the pan. Sprinkle ⅔ of the topping over the batter. Scoop the remaining batter over the topping and distribute evenly. Sprinkle with the remaining topping.
7. Bake until the tester inserted in the center comes out clean (30-45 minutes for the cake and 15 minutes for the miniature muffins). Cool on a wire rack for 20 minutes before removing from the pan. Serve warm or room temperature. If wrapped well and left at room temperature or refrigerated, this will keep for up to 3 days, and, if frozen, 2 months.

Yield: 1, 8-10-inch diameter coffee cake or 48 miniature muffins. Preparation time: 30 minutes. Cooking time varies.

Pumpkin Granola Muffins

IF YOU HAVE A JAR OF MY GRANOLA in your cupboard, these delicious, wholesome, crunchy muffins will only take minutes to make. See my Gluten-Free Nutty Granola recipe.

For the Muffins

½ cup unbleached all-purpose flour
¼ cup whole wheat pastry flour
¼ teaspoon baking soda
½ teaspoon baking powder
1 tablespoon pumpkin spice
⅛ teaspoon kosher salt
½ cup (¼ pound) unsalted butter, room temperature
½ cup white sugar
2 large eggs
6 tablespoons pumpkin purée
¾ cup granola, finely ground in nut grinder
½ cup raisins

Nutty Granola Topping

¼ cup granola, finely ground

Tips

- Use my nutty granola recipe for these muffins.
- Use the fine setting of a nut grinder to grind one cup of granola.

1. Preheat oven to 350° F (180° C). Prepare pan.

2. Combine flours, baking soda, baking powder, and kosher salt in a small bowl. Set aside.

3. Put the butter in the bowl of a standing mixer, and cream on high for 15 seconds. Add the sugar and vanilla and mix on high until light and fluffy, about 30 seconds. Add the eggs, 1 at a time, mixing on high, briefly after each addition. Add the vanilla and mix again. Scrape down the sides of the bowl using a rubber spatula and beat again for a few seconds on medium.

4. Add the flour mixture and pumpkin ⅓ at a time, beginning and ending with the dry ingredients. Mix on low after each addition, until just combined. Using a rubber spatula, scrape down the sides of the bowl to make sure all the flour has been absorbed.

5. Grind 1 cup granola (¾ cup for muffin and ¼ cup for topping). Set aside ¼ cup for the topping. Gently stir the ¾ cup ground granola and ½ cup raisins into the batter.

6. Fill each muffin cup ⅔ full. Sprinkle with the topping. Bake until a tester inserted into the center comes out clean (18 minutes for standard and 12 for miniature muffins).

7. Cool in the pan on a wire rack for 10 minutes. Serve warm or room temperature. Wrapped well, these will keep for up to 3 days at room temperature and 2 months in the freezer.

Yield: 8 standard-size or 24 miniature muffins. Preparation time: 15 minutes, if granola is pre-made. Cooking time varies.

Pumpkin Oatmeal Double Streusel Muffins

THE TENDER CHEWINESS of the nutritious old-fashioned rolled oats is texturally delightful and unusual in most pumpkin bread recipes. The muffins are even more irresistible with chocolate chips. They taste best the first two days after baking, but can be wrapped well and frozen for 3 to 4 weeks.

For the Muffins

1 cup whole wheat pastry flour
½ cup unbleached all-purpose flour
1 cup old-fashioned (not quick) rolled oats
¾ cup packed light brown sugar
1 tablespoon baking powder
1 heaping tablespoon pumpkin pie spice
1 teaspoon cinnamon
⅛ teaspoon cloves
½ teaspoon baking soda
¼ teaspoon sea salt
½ cup chopped pecans or walnuts (optional)
1 cup pumpkin purée
¾ cup whole or low-fat milk
⅓ cup vegetable oil
1 medium-large egg, slightly beaten
⅓-½ cups semisweet chocolate chips (optional)

Oat Streusel Topping

2 tablespoons unsalted butter (melted)
2 tablespoons packed brown sugar
1 heaping teaspoon pumpkin spice
½ cup old-fashioned rolled oats

Melt butter. Add brown sugar, pumpkin spice, and mix. Stir in rolled oats.
Choose a second recipe from the Toppings recipes for the middle of the muffin.

Variations & Tips

- I always take some prepared streusel topping from my freezer to add to the middle of these muffins to enhance the flavor and texture. Sprinkle about 1 tablespoon over the middle of each, top with remaining batter and finish with the Oat Streusel topping. If you prefer, just sprinkle the streusel on top of the muffin.
- Use a high-quality pumpkin purée (NOT pumpkin pie filling). There are many available. Two that I can recommend are Trader Joe's organic and Libby's.
- Pumpkin spice can be purchased premixed or made by combining ½ teaspoon ground cinnamon, ¼ teaspoon ground ginger, ⅛ teaspoon ground nutmeg and ⅛ teaspoon ground allspice. Proportions may be changed to suit your taste.

1. Preheat oven to 400° F (200° C). Prepare pan(s).

2. Combine the dry ingredients in a large mixing bowl. Measure the milk and oil into a 2-cup or larger liquid measuring cup. Add the pumpkin purée to the milk and oil and mix gently; add the egg and mix again.

3. Pour the wet mixture into the bowl of dry ingredients. Stir everything with either a spatula or large wood spoon just until moistened. Add the chocolate chips and stir again.

4. Prepare the topping. Melt butter. Add brown sugar, pumpkin spice and mix. Stir in rolled oats. For a second optional topping, take any other you have in the freezer (or make one from the Toppings recipes).

5. Fill muffin cups ⅓ with batter. (Optional: Evenly disperse 1 tablespoon of a crumb streusel topping over each.) Cover this topping with the remainder of the batter. Sprinkle all the Oat Streusel topping over the muffins.

6. Muffins are done (22 minutes for jumbo and 17 minutes for standard-size) when a tester inserted in the center comes out dry.

7. Serve warm or room temperature.

Yield: 6 jumbo or 10 standard-size muffins. Preparation time: 20 minutes. Cooking time varies.

Raisin Bran Muffins

THE SEARCH FOR THE PERFECT bran muffin ended the moment I tasted my adaptation. It has everything that I had been looking for, a dense, chewy texture and distinctive subtle flavors and sweetness. Plus, the batter can be used immediately or kept refrigerated for up to 3 days. As with most bran muffins, when well-wrapped, they are best eaten the day or within a few days after they are made. Do not refrigerate or freeze.

For the Muffins

1 cup unbleached all-purpose flour
⅔ cup plus 1 tablespoon and 1 teaspoon whole wheat pastry flour
1-⅓ teaspoon baking soda
2 teaspoons cinnamon
1 teaspoon nutmeg
¾ teaspoon sea salt
¾ cup raisins
1-½ cups plus 2 tablespoons wheat bran
⅔ cup plus 2 tablespoons boiling water
⅔ cup unsweetened applesauce
⅓ cup buttermilk
3 tablespoons canola oil
1 large egg
3 tablespoons plus 1-½ teaspoons molasses
⅓ cup packed light brown sugar
⅓ cup white sugar

Variations & Tips

- You may substitute 1 cup fresh blueberries for raisins. Rinse, dry and lightly dust them with all-purpose flour prior to gently stirring into the batter.
- My Carrot Bran Muffin is a variation of this recipe.
- If there is not enough batter for all the cups, fill the empty ones ½ full of water. This allows all muffins to rise evenly.

1. Preheat oven to 375° F (190° C). Place paper muffin cups in the muffin tin.

2. Mix all-purpose flour, whole wheat pastry flour, baking soda, cinnamon, nutmeg, sea salt, and raisins together in a medium-size bowl. Set aside.

3. Put the bran into a standing mixer bowl. Add boiling water and stir. Add the applesauce, buttermilk, oil, egg, and molasses and mix on low until incorporated. Scrape down sides of bowl. Add brown and white sugars and mix until combined. Scrape down.

4. Add the remaining dry ingredients (with the raisins) to the wet mixture. Gently mix with a large rubber spatula, scraping down the sides and bottom of the bowl to make sure all of the flour has been absorbed. Mix on low for 10 seconds.

5. With a large soup-size spoon, scoop the batter directly into the muffin cups until each is no more than ⅔ full. Bake until the tester inserted in the center comes out clean, just dry and not pasty (25-30 minutes for jumbo; 21-25 minutes for standard-size; 12-15 minutes for miniatures).

6. Serve warm or room temperature.

Yield: 6 jumbo, 10 standard-size, or 36 miniature muffins. Preparation time: 35 minutes. Cooking time varies. Batter keeps in refrigerator.

Drop Scones with Lemon, Poppyseeds, Jam, and Walnuts

FLOUR, BUTTER, SWEETENER, buttermilk, cream, baking soda, baking powder and salt are basic ingredients in most scones. Nearly all scone recipes are a variation on this theme. Their trademark flaky, solid yet delicate texture is achieved by lightly mixing the ingredients together. These jam-filled "drops" are perfect eaten warm on their own, without embellishment. But, they are also delicious served with butter and preserves. The dough can be used immediately or kept wrapped in plastic in the refrigerator for up to 2 days. For my wheat-free adaptation, see the Gluten-Free Drop Scones recipe.

For the Dough

½ pound (2 sticks) cold, unsalted butter, cut into ½-inch cubes
2-½ cups cold unbleached all-purpose flour
1 cup cold whole wheat pastry flour
¾ cup white sugar
1 teaspoon sea salt
1 teaspoon baking powder
½ teaspoon baking soda
Zest (chopped) from 2 large lemons
¾ cup chopped walnuts
2 tablespoons poppyseeds
¾ cup buttermilk
¼ cup maple syrup
½ cup cold cream
¾-1 cup jam of your choice

For the Topping

2 tablespoons cream
2 egg yolks

Variations & Tips

- Try honey or agave in place of maple syrup.
- Add ½-1 teaspoon ginger spice to the dry ingredients.
- Leave out the jam.
- Cold ingredients make a light, flaky scone.
- Do not completely cover the jam with dough. It is appealing to see some jam ooze out when baked.
- If batter has been kept in the refrigerator prior to baking, remove it 1 hour prior to shaping and baking the scones. Place 1-inch apart on pan.

1. Preheat oven to 400° F (200° C). Line the baking sheet with parchment paper.

2. Cut the cold butter into ½-inch cubes and freeze. Whisk together the all-purpose flour, whole wheat pastry flour, sugar, sea salt, baking powder, baking soda, lemon zest, walnuts, and poppyseeds in a large bowl. Scatter the cold butter over these dry ingredients and mix in with either a pastry cutter or 2 knives held together, until it resembles a coarse mixture with pea-size lumps of butter.

3. Whisk together the buttermilk, maple syrup, and ½ cup cream in a small bowl. With either a rubber spatula or wooden spoon, pour this into the flour mixture, and stir just till the dough holds together and no crumbs remain. The batter will be very crumbly with some dry ingredients stubbornly resting on the bottom of the bowl. This is fine.

4. Scoop mounds of batter into a ⅓-cup. Pack lightly with the back of a spoon until level. Drop mounds onto prepared baking sheet, using a knife to ease out batter. Place your thumb and forefinger in a semi-circle around the circumference of the scone. Push any crumbs into the mound. Then firmly press a teaspoon atop each scone, making a tablespoon-size indentation. Fill each with about 1 tablespoon jam. Using your fingers, push some dough from the sides of the mounds to just cover the preserves.

5. Prepare the topping. Mix 2 tablespoons cream with the 2 egg yolks. Brush this over the tops of the scones with a pastry brush. Bake 18-21 minutes, until golden brown.

6. Serve warm or room temperature. Scones are best eaten within 2 days of baking, and refreshed by baking at 350° F for 5 minutes. They may also be wrapped individually in plastic and frozen for up to 1 month.

Yield: 16 scones. Preparation time: 25 minutes. Cooking time: 18-21 minutes. Batter keeps in refrigerator.

Sour Cream Coffee Cake

EVERYONE WHO BAKES HAS ONE favorite version of a sour cream coffee cake. This is mine. It is not dissimilar from my grandmother Frances's recipe, written by hand nearly 100 years ago. But mine has benefited from continual improvements. These include adding spices, healthy whole wheat flour, and, if available, mesquite flour.

For the Cake
1 cup unbleached all-purpose flour
1 cup whole wheat pastry flour
1 teaspoon baking powder
1 teaspoon baking soda
½ teaspoon sea salt
1 teaspoon cinnamon
¼ teaspoon ground cloves
½ teaspoon each nutmeg, coriander and cardamom
½ cup (1 stick or 4 ounces) unsalted butter, room temperature
½ cup packed light brown sugar
¼ cup white sugar
2 medium-large eggs
1 cup plain, low-fat or whole Greek-style yogurt or sour cream

Simple Streusel Topping
3 tablespoons cold unsalted butter
2 tablespoons packed light brown sugar
2 tablespoons white sugar
6 tablespoons unbleached all-purpose flour
½ teaspoon cinnamon
½–¾ cup ground pecans or walnuts (optional)

1. Preheat oven to 350° F (180° C). Prepare pan(s).

2. Mix together flours, baking soda and powder, sea salt, and spices in a medium-size bowl. (If using fruit, rinse and pat dry with a paper towel.) Set aside dry ingredients and fruit.

3. Prepare topping. In a medium-size bowl, cut together butter and sugars with a pastry cutter (or 2 knives held together) until crumbly. Add flour and cinnamon and gently mix with fork. Add nuts and mix. Set aside.

4. Put butter and sugar in a standing mixer bowl. Blend well at medium speed. Add eggs one at a time and mix. Scrape down the sides of the bowl using a rubber spatula. Add sour cream or yogurt and mix on medium until combined. Scrape down sides of bowl.

5. Add dry ingredients to the bowl, ⅓ at a time, mixing on low until the flour is just integrated. Scrape down the sides of the bowl and stir until uniformly blended. (If using fruit, sprinkle with a few teaspoons all-purpose flour, add to the batter, and stir gently.)

6. Scoop ½ the batter into the pan and spread evenly with an inverted spatula. Cover with ⅔ of the topping, then with remaining batter. Finish by sprinkling the remaining topping evenly on top.

7. Bake until tester inserted in the center comes out clean (40 minutes for cake, 15 for miniature muffins). Serve warm or room temperature. If wrapped well and refrigerated, keeps for up to 2 days, and, if frozen, 2 months.

Variations & Tips

- Instead of 1 cup all-purpose and 1 cup whole wheat pastry flour, try using ½ cup mesquite, ¾ cup all-purpose, and ¾ cup whole wheat pastry flour.
- Experiment with adding seasonal fruits to the batter: 2 roughly-peeled apples or pears, 1 cup blueberries, or 1 cup raspberries. Just before using, dust fruit with 1 teaspoon all-purpose flour to prevent sinking.
- Try adding ⅓-½ cup semisweet chocolate chips or good quality, roughly chopped chocolate instead of fruit.
- This recipe is outstanding with apples pan-fried in French apple brandy Calvados. (See *Apple Stir Fry* recipe.)
- Breads with fruit take a little longer to cook.
- Greek style yogurt has a thick texture. I sometimes use it or lowfat sour cream.

Yield: 1 cake, 8-10-inch diameter, or 36 miniature muffins. Preparation time: 40 minutes. Cooking time varies.

Upside-Down Rhubarb (or Apple) Breakfast Cake

THIS CAKE CAN BE MADE WITH many different fruits. I usually use whatever is in season, but my favorites are rhubarb and apple. Rhubarb is a cool season vegetable, often prepared and eaten much like fruit. There are two common types: one, a balanced, mellow-flavored green and another tarter variety with deep red stalks. Both have a wonderful sweet, tart taste. If not in season, frozen sugar-free cut rhubarb is available in many grocery stores. For this cake, I use a round cast iron pan because it heats evenly, lasts a lifetime and is inexpensive.

For the Cake

¾ cup whole wheat pastry flour
½ cup unbleached all-purpose flour
¼ cup almond meal
½ teaspoon sea salt
1 teaspoon cinnamon
1-½ teaspoons baking powder
1 tablespoon finely grated orange zest
¼ pound unsalted butter, room temperature
¾ cup white sugar
2 large eggs
1 tablespoon Grand Marnier (Cointreau or orange extract)
1 cup low or full-fat sour cream, or Greek yogurt

For the Fruit

Rhubarb topping:
3 tablespoons unsalted butter
⅔ cup packed light brown sugar
1-½ pounds (3 cups) fresh or 12-ounce package of frozen rhubarb
Apple topping (alternative to rhubarb):
3 pounds (4 cups) tart apples, peeled, cored and cut lengthwise into ¾ inch wedges at the thickest part
1 teaspoon cinnamon
1 tablespoon lemon juice
½ cup packed light brown sugar

Toss apples with cinnamon and lemon juice in a large bowl. When ready to use, scoop out. Do not use remaining juices.

1. Preheat oven to 350° F (180° C). Prepare pan.

2. Combine flours, almond meal, sea salt, cinnamon, baking powder, and zest in a medium-size bowl. Set aside.

3. Prepare rhubarb topping. Wash, trim, and cut rhubarb diagonally into ¾-inch pieces and set aside. Melt 3 tablespoons unsalted butter in a well-seasoned, 10-inch diameter cast iron skillet over moderate heat until the foam subsides. Reduce the heat to low. Sprinkle ⅔ cup brown sugar evenly over the butter and heat. Leave undisturbed for 3 minutes. (All the brown sugar will not melt.) Remove the skillet from the heat, and arrange the rhubarb, cut sides down, in one layer over the brown sugar.

4. Mix the ¼ pound butter and ¾ cup white sugar in the bowl of a standing mixer on medium until light and fluffy. Scrape down the sides with a rubber spatula.

5. Add the eggs, 1 at a time, beating on medium until just blended. Scrape down the sides. Add Grand Marnier (Cointreau or orange extract) and beat on medium for a few seconds. Scrape down sides.

6. With mixer on low, add ⅓ flour mixture alternately with sour cream, beginning and ending with the flour. After each addition, beat on low until just combined, and scrape down the sides of the bowl. Cover the rhubarb evenly with the batter, being careful not to disturb the fruit.

 Yield: 1, 10-inch diameter cake serves 8. Preparation time: 35 minutes. Cooking time: 30-35 minutes in cast iron pan.

Upside-Down Nut Sprinkle Topping
⅔ cup chopped pecans
3 tablespoons sugar (½ white, ½ light brown)
1 teaspoon ground cinnamon

Variations & Tips

- If you substitute thin apple slices for rhubarb, use lemon zest instead of orange, and Calvados brandy or pure vanilla extract in place of Grand Marnier, Cointreau or orange extract.
- I buy small 50 milliliter bottles of liqueur for baking. These are available in liquor and grocery stores.
- This cake is perfect for breakfast, as well as for an afternoon snack with tea or coffee.
- Rhubarb is available in markets and larger grocery stores. The stalks should be heavy and crisp with tight, shiny skin and not rubbery, dry or fibrous. Wash the stalks, trim and discard the leaves and dry ends. (Resist the temptation to peel the fibrous, flavorful skin.) Store in loose plastic in the crisper drawer of your refrigerator. When not in season, use frozen rhubarb. This should not be defrosted prior to using.

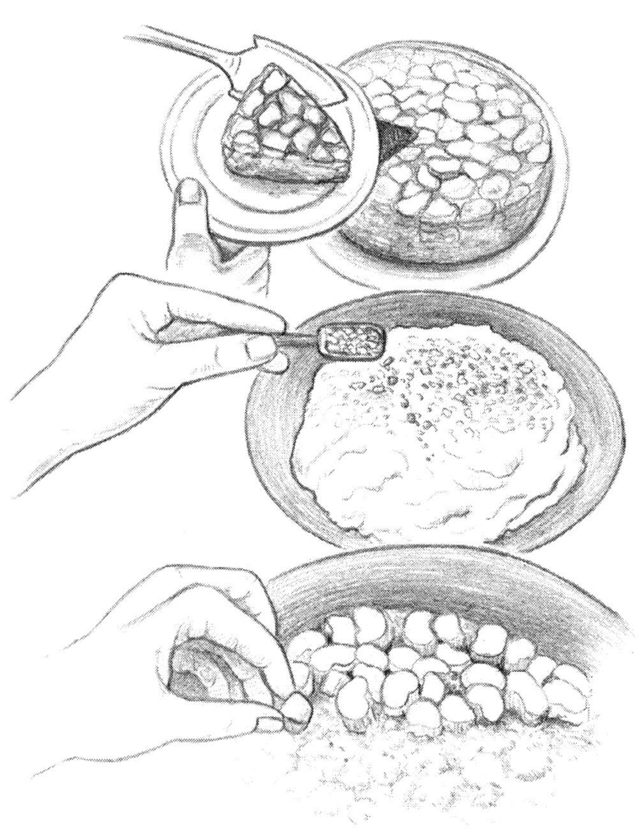

7. Prepare Nut Sprinkle topping. Mix all the ingredients together in a small bowl and sprinkle it over the top of the cake. Bake until a tester inserted in the center comes out clean (about 30 minutes). Cool in the skillet atop a wire rack for 20 minutes. To remove the cake from the pan, run a thin knife around the inside edge of the skillet. Invert a plate over the skillet. Press the plate and skillet together tightly while inverting the cake onto the plate. Carefully remove the skillet. Serve warm or room temperature. Store in the refrigerator and eat within 3 days of cooking.

Walnut Raisin Muffins

THE NUTTY TASTE OF THE WALNUTS shines through as soon as you bite into this simple muffin. Maybe it is the overall nutritional quality of walnuts that impresses my palate. Scientific studies have undisputedly touted the benefits of nuts in a diet, with walnuts coming out on top. They have also been attributed to helping to treat some diseases, including diabetes. Buttermilk is ideal in baking, adding a rich flavor and little fat to baked goods. I always plump raisins when I bake. They taste so much sweeter that way. If you do not plump them, they will soak up moisture from the recipe.

For the Muffins

⅔ cup raisins plus 2 tablespoons warm water, orange juice, or rum
⅔ cup unsalted butter, melted and cooled
1 cup packed light brown sugar
⅔ cup buttermilk or low-fat yogurt
1 tablespoon pure vanilla extract
1 heaping teaspoon cinnamon
3 medium-large eggs
1 cup unbleached all-purpose flour
¾ cup whole wheat pastry flour
¼ teaspoon baking soda
1-½ teaspoons baking powder
¼ teaspoon kosher salt

Walnut Crumb Topping

1 cup chopped walnuts
6 tablespoons unbleached all-purpose flour
½ stick (4 tablespoons) unsalted, cold butter, cut in cubes
2 tablespoons packed dark brown sugar
½ teaspoon cinnamon
¼ teaspoon kosher salt

1. Preheat oven to 350° F (180° C). Prepare pan(s).

2. Empty the raisins into a small bowl. Barely cover them with warm or hot water, or with another liquid of your choice. Let stand for at least 10 minutes or more.

3. Melt the ⅔ cup butter on low. Set aside to cool.

4. In the bowl of a standing mixer, whisk sugar, buttermilk or yogurt, vanilla, and cinnamon on low until incorporated. Add eggs, one at a time, whisking on low until blended.

5. In a medium-size bowl, gently whisk the all-purpose flour, whole wheat pastry flour, baking soda, baking powder, and kosher salt. Add to the wet ingredients, mixing on low until the dry ingredients almost disappear. With a large rubber spatula, scrape down the sides and bottom of the bowl, making sure all the flour is absorbed. Fold the drained raisins into the batter, then the butter, in thirds, stirring with a rubber spatula after each addition.

6. Prepare topping. In medium-size bowl, combine 4 tablespoons cubed butter and 2 tablespoons dark brown sugar. With pastry cutter (or 2 knives held together), cut in the butter until the mixture resembles coarse crumbs. Add flour, kosher salt, and walnuts and mix gently with a fork. Set aside.

7. Scoop ½ the batter, then ½ the topping into the muffin cups. Finish with remaining batter, then remaining topping until each is no more than ⅔ full. Bake until the tester inserted in the center comes out clean, just dry and not pasty (23 minutes for jumbo; 19 minutes for standard).

8. Serve warm or room temperature. Wrapped well and refrigerated, this keeps for 3 days in the refrigerator and 2 months frozen.

Yield: 6 jumbo or 10 standard-size muffins. Preparation time: 30 minutes. Cooking time varies.

Variations & Tips

- Plump raisins in warm water, juice, rum, or liquor. Drain before adding to the batter.
- If you do not have buttermilk in your refrigerator, you can easily make it using milk and white vinegar or lemon: place 1 tablespoon of either vinegar or lemon into a liquid measuring cup; add enough milk, preferably at room temperature, to bring the liquid up to the 1-cup line; mix and let stand 5 minutes. If any remains, store it in the refrigerator.
- Try mixing ¾ cup plain yogurt with ¼ cup milk to make 1 cup of buttermilk substitute.
- If you want to substitute buttermilk for milk in a recipe, you must also change the amount of baking soda and baking powder. Because of the higher acid content in buttermilk, you will usually need less baking soda or baking powder. For each cup of buttermilk substituted for milk, use 2 teaspoons less baking powder and ½ teaspoon more baking soda.
- Kosher salt has large, irregularly-shaped flakes that dissolve easily. Because of the large surface area, it imparts flavor with less risk of oversalting. (¾ teaspoon kosher salt equals 1 teaspoon sea salt.)

Six Gluten-Free Recipes

Being Gluten-Free

GLUTEN CAUSES ILLNESS IN PEOPLE WITH celiac disease, a chronic condition that results in damage to the lining of the small intestine and prevents it from absorbing parts of food that are important for staying healthy. The damage is due to a reaction to eating gluten, which is found in wheat and other grains. Some celiacs may have adverse reactions to naturally gluten-free products. Thus, many producers have taken additional steps to ensure purity in the products they label. (See Glossary – The Twenty-One Ingredients in Detail, number 7, Non-gluten forming flours.)

For those who want to bake a simple gluten-free recipe from scratch, I recommend using one of the many available all-purpose gluten-free flours and add guar gum or xanthan gum to bind the gluten-free ingredients. (If you do not add one of these, your gluten-free baked good would likely end up as a pile of crumbs.) There are also some good gluten-free baking mixes that are new to the market.

I have included 6 gluten-free recipes in **Baking Breakfast** for that family member or guest who is gluten-intolerant. Many of the traditional recipes in this collection can be adapted to gluten-free by substituting an all-purpose, gluten-free flour for flour with wheat.

Gluten-Free Buttermilk Biscuits with Shredded Cheese and Herb

IN THIS VERSION of my Buttermilk Biscuits, I use gluten-free, all-purpose flour and whole grain oat flour in place of wheat, and add guar gum or xanthan gum as a binding agent.

For the Bread

10 tablespoons cold unsalted butter
¾ cup whole grain oat flour (certified free of cross-contamination)
1-½ cups gluten-free, all-purpose baking flour
1-½ teaspoons xanthan gum or guar gum
2 teaspoons baking powder
½ teaspoon baking soda
1 teaspoon sea salt
1 cup shredded Parmesan cheese
2 teaspoons chopped fresh rosemary
1 cup cold buttermilk

Variations & Tips

- Substitute any hard cheese and herb for the Parmesan and rosemary. There are infinite possibilities: cheddar, Gruyère, Gouda, thyme and chives.
- Cover the unbaked biscuits (either prior to or after cutting into rounds) with plastic wrap, and refrigerate overnight or freeze for up to 1 month.
- The colder the butter and buttermilk, the flakier the biscuits. The small pieces of butter in the dough contribute to the flakiness.
- The higher the quality of cheese, the better the biscuit. For instance, I always use Parmigiano-Reggiano, because of its dependable outstanding quality. (Italian law mandates that cheese with this name be made in specific districts using a prescribed recipe. Parmesan is not included and is usually made outside Italy.)

1. Position a rack in the middle of the oven. Preheat oven to 425° F (215° C). Line the baking sheet with parchment paper.

2. Cut the butter into ½-inch cubes and chill.

3. Combine the oat flour, gluten-free flour, xanthan gum, baking powder, baking soda, and sea salt in a large bowl. Cut in the cold butter, using a pastry cutter or 2 knives, until the mixture looks like coarse meal. Add Parmesan and rosemary and mix briefly with a fork. Then pour in the cold buttermilk and continue to stir with a fork until the dry ingredients are evenly moist.

4. Lightly flour the counter/work surface with either oat or gluten-free flour; turn out the dough and pat it, just until it comes together, into a ½-¾ inch thick circle. (If the dough is too moist, it will stick to the counter. Sprinkle a few more teaspoons of flour onto the counter; reshape the circle as you pat it into the flour.)

5. Wrap the dough in wax or plastic wrap and chill for at least 30 minutes prior to or the night before baking. Cut into rounds using a 2-½ inch diameter cookie cutter, glass, or canning jar band. Reassemble the scraps and cut or shape them as well.

6. Place biscuits 1-inch apart on baking sheet and cook (15 minutes), until golden brown. Serve warm or room temperature. These keep for a few days, and taste best warmed for 5 minutes in a 350° F oven. Do not freeze the baked biscuits. Instead, prior to baking, freeze them in a single layer, wrapped and sealed in a plastic bag for 1 month or in the refrigerator for 24 hours. Bake directly from cooler and add a few minutes to the baking time.

Yield: 20, 2-½-inch round biscuits. Preparation time: 20 minutes. Cooking time: 15 minutes. Dough keeps in refrigerator and freezer.

Gluten-Free Granola Breakfast Bars

THESE BREAKFAST BARS are a variation on my granola recipe. Instead of oil, I substitute unsalted butter. I make them a little sweeter by gluing them together with brown sugar and more honey. When done cooking, cut the granola into 20 bars, or whatever size you like. Then, cool and wrap individually in plastic wrap, or in an airtight container between sheets of wax paper so they don't stick together. Store in an airtight container for up to a week or the freezer for up to a few months.

For the Bars

2 cups old-fashioned (not quick) certified gluten-free rolled oats
½ cup raw or dry-roasted pepita (pumpkin) seeds
½ cup sesame seeds
½ cup raw or dry-roasted sunflower seeds
½ cup raw or dry-roasted chopped almonds
½ cup raw or dry-roasted chopped cashews
½ cup unsweetened shredded coconut
¼ cup raw or dry-roasted wheat germ
Dash or 2 of cinnamon
⅓ cup (or 4 tablespoons plus 1-½ teaspoons) unsalted butter
½ cup honey of your choice
¼ cup packed dark brown sugar
Heaping tablespoon of unsweetened, unsalted peanut butter (optional)
6 ounces chopped dried fruit of your choice, such as raisins, apricots, apples, apricots, or cherries
4 ounces chopped semisweet chocolate (optional)

Variations & Tips

- Sometimes I add good-quality, semisweet chocolate chips or chopped chunks, after the granola has cooled.
- It is easy to grab one for work or school when they are individually wrapped.

1. Preheat oven to 350° F (180° C). Line a cookie sheet with sides and a lightly buttered 9 x 9-inch glass baking dish with parchment paper. Set them aside. In a medium bowl, mix the oats; pepita, sesame, and sunflower seeds; almonds; cashews; coconut; and wheat germ, plus cinnamon. Spread onto the cookie sheet and place in the oven until light brown (about 15 minutes).

2. Meanwhile, combine the butter, honey, brown sugar, and peanut butter in a medium saucepan over medium heat. Cook until the brown sugar has completely dissolved.

3. When the oat mixture is done, remove it from the oven and reduce the heat to 300° F (160° C). Immediately add the oat mixture to the liquid. Mix very well to make sure the "glue" gets over everything. (Optional: If you choose, now add dried fruit or chocolate and stir to combine.)

4. Turn mixture out onto the prepared baking dish and evenly distribute by pressing down with the back of a spatula. Spread out the mixture with a wooden spoon or spatula.

5. Bake for 20 minutes, until light brown. Remove from oven and cool in pan, on a cooling rack for 15 minutes. While in pan, cut into 20 bars. Cool to room temperature, about one hour more. Then, hold onto the parchment and lift bars from the pan and onto a large cutting board. Using a sharp knife, recut the bars along the original cuts.

Yield: 20, 2 x 2-½ inch bars. Preparation time: 25 minutes. Cooking time: 20 minutes.

Gluten-Free Nutty Granola

THIS GRANOLA HAS THE PERFECT CRUNCH. It is high in iron, fiber, and protein. Use it as a bread or muffin topping, mixed into batter before baking; over yogurt and fresh fruit, or as cereal with milk. It's also a great snack for any time of day. Make it your own by including different ingredients. Try adding raisins, or other chopped fruits after it cools.

For the Nutty Granola

¼ cup vegetable oil
¼ cup honey
Heaping tablespoon of unsweetened, unsalted peanut butter (optional)
2 cups old-fashioned (not quick) certified gluten-free rolled oats
½ cup raw or dry-roasted pepita (pumpkin) seeds
½ cup raw or dry-roasted sesame seeds
½ cup raw or dry-roasted sunflower seeds
½ cup raw or dry-roasted chopped almonds
½ cup unsweetened shredded coconut
½ cup raw or dry-roasted chopped cashews
¼ cup raw or dry-roasted wheat germ
Dash or 2 of cinnamon
Dried fruit of your choice, such as raisins, apricots, and/or apples (optional)

Variations & Tips

- Granola tastes best when you use nuts and seeds that are unsalted, and raw or dry roasted.
- Substitute the almonds and cashews with other favorite nuts and the peanut butter with almond butter.
- Substitute rolled oats that are not certified gluten-free if you are gluten tolerant.
- Prior to measuring honey, pour the smallest drop of oil into the bottom of the measuring cup. This way, the honey will not stick to the cup, but will easily slide out.

1. Preheat oven to 250° F (120° C). Line the bottom of a large sheet pan, which has low sides, with parchment paper.
2. Pour the oil, then the honey, and last the peanut butter into a transparent measuring cup. Microwave on low for less than 1 minute and stir to mix. Set aside.
3. Add all of the dry ingredients to a large bowl and mix.
4. Pour the wet ingredients into the dry and mix thoroughly with a rubber spatula or a large wood spoon. Spread the granola onto the prepared pan, press with a large cooking spatula, and place in the preheated oven.
5. After 30 minutes, remove the pan from the oven and turn over the granola with the cooking spatula.
6. Cook for 30-40 minutes longer, until the granola is medium brown.
7. Cool in the cookie sheet atop a cooling rack. (Optional: Add dried fruit to the cool granola.) The granola keeps for a few weeks stored in an airtight container.

Yield: 6 cups granola. Preparation time: 15 minutes. Cooking time: 60 minutes.

Gluten-Free Mesquite Almond Tea Cake

THIS IS A GLUTEN-FREE, dairy-free version of the Mesquite Almond Tea Cake. It is more complex than my other gluten-free recipes because, instead of using the all-purpose, gluten-free flour, I substitute common components of such flour. I use tapioca flour as a binding agent, and xanthan gum or guar gum as a binding and thickening agent. Eggs are not a dairy product or a derivative of dairy products. Thus, unless specifically allergic to them, those with milk allergies or who are lactose intolerant can eat eggs.

For the Cake

½ cup mesquite meal
2 tablespoons amaranth flour
6 tablespoons brown rice flour
½ cup almond meal
¼ cup tapioca flour
2 teaspoons xanthan gum or guar gum
1 teaspoon baking powder
¼ teaspoon sea salt
½ cup agave nectar
¼ cup canola oil
¾ cup soy, rice or almond milk
2 small or 1 large egg
1 teaspoon pure vanilla extract
1 teaspoon pure almond extract

Variations & Tips

- Substitute the 2 tablespoons amaranth flour with brown rice flour.
- Substitute half of the agave with maple syrup.

1. Preheat oven to 350° F (180° C). Prepare pan(s).
2. Sift mesquite, amaranth, brown rice, almond meal, tapioca, xanthan or guar gum, baking powder, and sea salt onto parchment or wax paper. Set aside.
3. Place the agave, oil, and milk into a large measuring cup and stir gently.
4. Break the egg(s) into a small cup and stir gently with a fork. Add to the wet mixture, along with the vanilla and almond extracts, and stir slightly. Pour into a standing mixer bowl.
5. Add the dry ingredients to the bowl, ¼ at a time, mixing on low until the flour is combined. Using a rubber spatula, scrape the sides of the bowl to make sure all the flour has been absorbed.
6. Pour or spoon the batter into the prepared pan(s), ⅔ full. Smooth the surface with an offset spatula. Then bake until the tester inserted in the center comes out clean (40-45 minutes for the bread pan; 30 minutes for the mini-loaf pans; 15 minutes for miniatures). Serve warm or room temperature. Wrapped well, this will keep up to 3 days, and, if frozen, 2 months.

Yield: 1, 9 x 5-inch loaf, 2 mini-loaves, or 36 miniature muffins. Preparation time: 20 minutes. Cooking time varies.

Gluten-Free Olive Oil and Orange Corn Cake

IF YOU LIKE OLIVE OIL, corn and orange, you will love this simple, delicious crunchy cake. The moist, dense texture is terrific and the orange peel and olive oil are an aromatic complement to each other. This is the perfect companion to a morning cup of tea or a strong cup of coffee.

For the Cake

1 cup gluten-free, coarsely-ground cornmeal
1 cup gluten-free, whole grain corn flour
1-¼ cups almond meal
2 teaspoons baking powder
¼ teaspoon sea salt
2 large eggs
¾ cup white sugar
Zest of 2 oranges
½ cup mild-flavored, fruity olive oil
½ cup whole milk
½ teaspoon almond extract

Variations & Tips

- For an even crunchier texture, substitute some or all of the corn flour with coarsely-ground cornmeal.
- For a less crunchy texture, substitute almond meal/flour for some or all of the almond meal.
- The labeling of ground almonds can be confusing. Some read *Almond Meal*, others *Almond Meal/Flour*. However, depending upon the mill, the almond meal/flour may have the same texture as the almond meal. In general, the meal/flour is skinless, blanched almonds that are finely ground.

1. Preheat oven to 350° F (180° C). Prepare pan(s).
2. Stir together the cornmeal, corn flour, almond meal, baking powder, and sea salt in a medium bowl. Set aside.
3. In a standing mixer bowl, whisk the eggs and sugar together until blended well and light color. Add the zest, olive oil, milk, and extract and mix until just combined. (Batter may be slightly lumpy.)
4. Pour the batter into the prepared pan(s) ⅔ full. Smooth the surface with an offset spatula. Bake until golden brown and the center is slightly moist, when a toothpick inserted in the middle comes out with a few crumbs (40-45 minutes for the bread pan and 25-30 minutes for the mini-loaf pans). Serve warm or room temperature. If wrapped well, it will keep for up to 3 days, and 2 months frozen.

Yield: 1, 9 X 5-inch loaf or 3 mini-loaves. Preparation time: 20 minutes. Cooking time varies.

Gluten-Free Drop Scones with Lemon, Poppyseeds, Jam, and Walnuts

IN THIS DELICIOUS GLUTEN-FREE version of my Drop Scones, I use gluten-free, all-purpose flour and almond meal in place of wheat, and add guar gum or xanthan gum to bind the gluten-free ingredients. The dough can be used immediately or kept wrapped in plastic in the refrigerator for up to 2 days.

For the Dough

½ pound (2 sticks) cold, unsalted butter, cut into ½-inch cubes
2-½ cups cold gluten-free all-purpose baking flour
1 cup cold almond nut meal
2-½ teaspoons xanthan gum or guar gum
¾ cup white sugar
1 teaspoon sea salt
1 teaspoon baking powder
½ teaspoon baking soda
Zest (chopped) from 2 large lemons
¾ cup chopped walnuts
2 tablespoons poppyseeds
¾ cup cold buttermilk
¼ cup maple syrup
½ cup cold cream
¾-1 cup jam of your choice

For the Topping

2 tablespoons cream
2 egg yolks

1. Preheat oven to 400° F (200° C). Line the baking sheet with parchment paper.

2. Cut the cold butter into ½-inch cubes and freeze. Whisk together the gluten-free flour, almond nut meal, xanthan gum, sugar, salt, baking powder, baking soda, lemon zest, walnuts, and poppyseeds in a large bowl. Scatter the cold butter over these dry ingredients and mix in with a pastry cutter (or 2 knives held together) until it resembles a coarse mixture with pea-size lumps of butter.

3. Whisk together the buttermilk, maple syrup, and ½ cup cream in a small bowl. With a rubber spatula or wooden spoon, pour into the dry mixture. Stir just till dough holds together and no crumbs remain.

4. Scoop mounds of batter into a ⅓-cup. Pack lightly with the back of a spoon until level. Drop mounds onto prepared baking sheet, using a knife to ease out batter. Place your thumb and forefinger in a semi-circle around the circumference of the scone. Push any crumbs into the mound. Then firmly press a teaspoon atop each scone, making a tablespoon-size indentation. Fill each with about 1 tablespoon jam. Using your fingers, push some dough from the sides of the mounds to just cover the preserves.

5. Prepare topping. Mix 2 tablespoons cream with the 2 egg yolks. Brush over the tops of the scones with a pastry brush. Bake 18-21 minutes, until golden brown.

6. Serve warm or room temperature. Scones are best eaten within 2 days of baking, and refreshed by baking at 350° F for 5 minutes. They may also be wrapped individually in plastic and frozen for up to 1 month.

Yield: 16 scones. Preparation time: 25 minutes. Cooking time: 18-21 minutes. Batter keeps in refrigerator.

Variations & Tips

- Try honey or agave in place of maple syrup.
- Add ½-1 teaspoon ginger spice to the dry ingredients.
- Leave out the jam.
- Cold ingredients make a light, flaky scone.
- Do not completely cover the jam with dough. It is appealing to see some jam ooze out when baked.
- If batter has been kept in the refrigerator prior to baking, remove it one hour prior to shaping and baking the scones. Place 1-inch apart on the pan.
- For cake, muffin, and quick bread recipes, add ½-¾ teaspoon guar gum or xanthan gum per cup of gluten-free flour.

Toppings

Toppings

I USE THE TERMS crumb topping and streusel topping interchangeably. In my recipes, I recommend a particular topping, but in most cases they may be substituted for one another. There are, also, many ways to experiment with these toppings. Mix it up by using different nuts or, for a more nutty richness, by replacing ⅓ of the white flour with almond meal. Each topping recipe is enough for one recipe. Freeze leftover toppings in a labeled plastic bag.

Apple Nut

I like this with Cereal Apple Muffins.

2 tablespoons and 1-½ teaspoons unsalted butter, melted
1 tablespoon and 1-½ teaspoons packed brown sugar
½ heaping teaspoon cinnamon
¼ cup chopped pecans or walnuts
¼ cup finely-chopped apples

In a small bowl, mix melted butter, sugar, cinnamon, nuts, and ¼ cup chopped apple together.

Crunchy Streusel

6 tablespoons unsalted cold butter (cut into tablespoons)
¾ cup packed light brown sugar
½ cup unbleached all-purpose flour
½ teaspoon sea salt
½ teaspoon cinnamon
¼ cup chopped walnuts (or any other favorite nut)
¼ cup old-fashioned rolled oats

In a medium-size bowl, combine butter and sugar. Using a pastry cutter (or 2 knives held together), cut until the mixture resembles coarse crumbs. Add the flour, salt, cinnamon, rolled oats, and walnuts; mix gently with a spoon.

Nutty Granola

I like this with Pumpkin Granola Muffins.

This granola has the perfect crunch. It is high in iron, fiber, and protein. Use it as a bread or muffin topping, over yogurt and fresh fruit, or as cereal with milk. It's also a great snack for any time of day. Make it your own by including different ingredients (see page 81 for suggested variations).

¼ cup vegetable oil
¼ cup honey
Heaping tablespoon of unsweetened, unsalted peanut butter (optional)
2 cups old-fashioned (not quick) rolled oats
½ cup raw or dry-roasted pepita (pumpkin) seeds
½ cup raw or dry-roasted sesame seeds
½ cup raw or dry-roasted sunflower seeds
½ cup raw or dry-roasted chopped almonds
½ cup unsweetened shredded coconut
½ cup raw or dry-roasted chopped cashews
¼ cup raw or dry-roasted wheat germ
Dash or 2 of cinnamon
Dried fruit of your choice, such as raisins, apricots, and/or apples

Preheat oven to 250° F (120° C). Line the bottom of a large, low-sided sheet pan with parchment paper. Pour the oil, then the honey, and, last, the peanut butter into a transparent measuring cup. Microwave on low for less than a minute and stir to mix. Set aside.

Add all of the dry ingredients to a large bowl and mix with either a rubber spatula or a large wood spoon. Pour the wet ingredients into the dry and mix thoroughly. Spread the granola onto the prepared pan, press with a large spatula, and place in the preheated oven.

After 30 minutes, remove the pan from the oven and turn over the granola with a large cooking spatula. Cook for 30-45 minutes longer, until the granola is light to medium brown. Cool in the cookie sheet atop a cooling rack. (Optional: Add dried fruit to the cool granola.) The granola keeps for a few weeks stored in an airtight container.

Nutty Streusel

5 tablespoons unsalted cold butter (cut into tablespoons)
¼ cup white sugar
⅓ cup packed light brown sugar
⅓ cup unbleached all-purpose flour
1 heaping teaspoon cinnamon
¼ teaspoon sea salt
½ cup chopped walnuts

With pastry cutter (or 2 knives held together), cut butter and sugar together until crumbly and pea-like. Combine flour, spice and salt, and gently stir into the butter/sugar with a fork. Stir in the nuts.

Oat Streusel

I like this with Pumpkin Oatmeal Double Streusel Muffins.

2 tablespoons unsalted butter (melted)
2 tablespoons packed light brown sugar
½ cup old-fashioned rolled oats
1 heaping teaspoon pumpkin spice

Melt butter. Add brown sugar, pumpkin spice, and mix. Stir in rolled oats.

Oatmeal Crunch

I like this with the Fruit Purée Pear Crunch Bread.

2 tablespoons unsalted butter
2 tablespoons packed brown sugar
½ teaspoon cinnamon
½ cup old-fashioned rolled oats

Melt butter. Add the brown sugar and cinnamon to the butter and combine. Add the rolled oats and mix thoroughly.

Pecan Spice

I like this with Apple Streusel Nut Bread and Oatmeal Apricot Muffins.

⅔ cup unbleached all-purpose flour
⅓ cup packed light brown sugar
1 heaping teaspoon cinnamon
3 tablespoons unsalted cold butter (cut into tablespoons)
⅔ cup chopped pecans

In a medium-size bowl, combine butter and sugar. With a pastry cutter (or 2 knives held together), cut together until the mixture resembles coarse crumbs. Add the flour, cinnamon, and pecans and mix gently with a fork.

Simple Pecan

I like this with Pecan Sour Cream Dream Cake.

¾ cup chopped pecans
2 tablespoons white sugar
2 tablespoons packed light brown sugar
1 heaping teaspoon ground cinnamon

Mix all together in a small bowl.

Simple Streusel

I like this with Sour Cream Coffee Cake.

3 tablespoons unsalted cold butter (cut into tablespoons)
¼ cup sugar (½ white, ½ light brown)
6 tablespoons unbleached all-purpose flour
1 heaping teaspoon cinnamon
½-¾ cup ground pecans or walnuts (optional)

With pastry cutter (or 2 knives held together), cut butter and sugar together until crumbly and pea-like. Combine flour and spices, and gently stir into butter/sugar with a fork.

Streusel Cinnamon
I like this with the Fruit Purée Banana Nut and Peach Nut Breads.

3 tablespoons cold unsalted butter
2 tablespoons packed light brown sugar
2 tablespoons white sugar
1 teaspoon cinnamon
6 tablespoons unbleached all-purpose flour
½ cup ground nuts (pecans and/or walnuts) (optional)

With a pastry cutter (or 2 knives held together), cut the cold butter with the brown and white sugars until the mixture is crumbly and pea-size. Add flour and cinnamon. Mix gently with a fork. (Optional: Add nuts.)

Traditional Streusel
I like this with Sour Cream Coffee Cake.

½ cup unbleached all-purpose flour
½ cup quick or old-fashioned rolled oats
⅓ cup sugar
½ teaspoon cinnamon
⅛ teaspoon sea salt
6 tablespoons unsalted cold butter (cubed)

In a medium-size bowl, mix the flour, oats, sugar, cinnamon, and salt. Add the butter and quickly rub it and the dry ingredients between your fingertips, squeezing to form clumps. Continue until the clumps of butter are small, uniform in size, and a little crumbly.

Upside-Down Nut Sprinkle
I like this with Upside-Down Rhubarb Breakfast Cake.

⅔ cup chopped pecans
3 tablespoons sugar (½ white, ½ light brown)
1 teaspoon ground cinnamon

Mix all together in a small bowl.

Walnut Chocolate Streusel
I like this with Peanut Butter Chip Muffins.

½ cup white sugar
¼ cup unsweetened cocoa powder
3 tablespoons cold, unsalted butter, cut into small pieces
¼ cup finely chopped walnuts

In medium-size bowl, combine sugar and cocoa. Use a fork to break up any hard pieces of cocoa. Add the pieces of butter to the sugary cocoa mixture. With pastry cutter (or 2 knives held together), cut in the butter until it resembles coarse crumbs. Add the walnuts and mix gently with a spoon.

Walnut Crumb
I like this with Walnut Raisin Muffins.

4 tablespoons unsalted cold butter (cubed)
2 tablespoons packed dark brown sugar
6 tablespoons unbleached all-purpose flour
½ teaspoon cinnamon
¼ teaspoon kosher salt
1 cup chopped walnuts

In medium-size bowl, combine butter and brown sugar. With a pastry cutter (or 2 knives held together), cut together until the mixture resembles coarse crumbs. Add flour, cinnamon, salt, and walnuts and mix gently with a fork.

Variations & Tips for Toppings

• In addition to cinnamon, add a few heavy shakes of one or more of the following spices: cardamom, ginger, allspice, nutmeg and coriander, and a light shake of cloves. Experiment with measurements.

• Sometimes butter should be cold and sometimes it should be room temperature. When a recipe calls for cutting butter into a dry ingredient for a coarse meal outcome, the butter must be cold. Keep butter in the refrigerator until you are ready to use it. To cool it down quickly, place the butter in the freezer for a short time. If butter is too soft, it will not form a coarse meal.

• Instead of cutting the butter into cubes, I sometimes shave frozen butter with a grater. The result is uniform pieces that combine easily with the rest of the topping ingredients.

• To simplify baking, from time to time I double the topping recipe, freeze, and save it for future use.

• I sometimes use different toppings for the center and top of a cake. If there are a few to choose from in my freezer, it makes baking easier.

Glossary

Twenty-One Ingredients to Have in Your Kitchen

THESE BASICS ARE ESSENTIAL to have on hand. I use them in many of my recipes.

1. Semisweet chocolate
2. Eggs
3. Extracts and liqueurs
4. Solid fat
5. Liquid fat
6. Gluten-forming flours
7. Non-gluten forming flours
8. Dry, fresh and frozen fruit
9. Leavening agents
10. Liquids (water, juice, milk, and buttermilk)
11. Nuts and seeds
12. Rolled oats
13. Sea salt
14. Sour cream
15. Spices
16. Dry sweeteners
17. Liquid sweeteners
18. Vinegar (white, apple, or rice)
19. Guar gum or xanthan gum
20. Yogurt
21. Lemon and orange zests

The Twenty-One Ingredients in Detail

HERE'S MORE INFORMATION about the 21 ingredients, descriptions of their flavors and consistencies, some advice about when to use them, and additional best practices.

1. Semisweet Chocolate

Good-quality chocolate has smooth texture, is rich and nicely balanced and tastes great. So, I always use good semisweet chocolate chips or bars for baking. Chocolate is made from roasted, crushed, and ground cacao beans. The types vary according to their sugar and cocoa solid content. Unsweetened contains no sugar and tastes bitter. Bittersweet and semisweet chocolates are dark, contain sugar and can be used interchangeably. Bittersweet has a little less sugar than semisweet, so the distinction between them is slight. Chocolate should be kept in a dry, cool place (but not the refrigerator) at 65° F (18° C), wrapped tightly in a few layers of plastic wrap, in a dark cupboard, and away from strong-smelling foods.

2. Eggs

Eggs serve many functions in baked goods. They add flavor and color (especially if they are fresh, free-range, and organic); contribute to structure; incorporate air when beaten; provide liquid, fat, and protein; and emulsify fat with liquid ingredients.

Tip: Eggs blend better and beat lighter if brought to room temperature for 20 minutes before using. A quick way to bring eggs to room temperature is to submerge them in warm tap water for 10-15 minutes.

Tip: Never add a hot ingredient to a mixture containing eggs.

Tip: Cakes made without the emulsifying action from the egg yolk may not have a uniform flavor and texture. Reducing or omitting egg yolks can result in less tenderness and volume. Unless otherwise specified, the best size egg to use is Grade A, large (2 ounce).

Tip: Break eggs into a cup and not directly into the batter. If you need to remove an eggshell, it is easier.

Tip: To remove a piece of eggshell from a cracked egg, scoop it up with a large piece of the shell.

3. Extracts and Liqueurs

Extracts are concentrated flavoring agents that are crucial to good baking. They add a given flavor to food without adding volume. Extracts are made either by dissolving a spice or a flavoring oil in alcohol. This works well for baking because the alcohol evaporates during cooking, leaving behind the flavoring. When stored in a cool, dark place with tight lids, extracts keep for a long time, though their flavor gradually diminishes. Common baking extracts include almond, lemon, orange, and vanilla.

Almond extract is made from pure almond oil. It has a strong, fragrant almond flavor. To make your own almond extract, combine vanilla extract with 4-8 times the amount of an almond liqueur, such as Amaretto. Use slightly more total extract. Use ½ teaspoon to replace 1 tablespoon almond liqueur.

Lemon extract has a strong lemon flavor and is used in baking to give the essence of lemon without the acid. It is made with lemon zest and vodka.

Pure orange extract may be hard to find. Therefore, you can make your own or use an orange liqueur, such as Grand Marnier or Cointreau. To make orange extract, combine orange juice plus minced orange zest. Reduce another liquid in the recipe to compensate for the orange juice. One teaspoon orange extract equals 2-3 tablespoons orange liqueur.

Vanilla extract is made from vanilla beans that have been steeped in alcohol. It is nutty and spicy, with complex flavors that have hints of honey and maple, licorice, and prune. Pure extract made with vanilla from the Bourbon Islands (which includes Madagascar) is well regarded. Mexican vanilla extract has a fine reputation, but there have been reports of its being adulterated.

Liqueurs. For more depth of flavor, I sometimes substitute liqueur for extract. Liqueurs are spirits with added sugar and added flavors from fruits, herbs, and nuts. They are often syrupy. (Liqueurs and liquors are not the same. Liquor is an alcoholic drink that is made from the fermentation of grains or other plants. It is not sugary sweet, even when infused with flavors.)

Tip: Use only pure extracts with no additives. An imitation or artificial extract is an inexpensive substitute for a pure extract. Even the best imitation extracts aren't quite as full-flavored and complex as real ones.

Tip: Because it is potent, recipes rarely call for more than 1 teaspoon extract. One teaspoon extract equals 1 tablespoon liqueur.

Tip: If a recipe calls for a liqueur that I seldom use, I buy the 50 milliliter (1.7 ounce) mini, airplane-size bottles.

4. Solid Fat

Whether in solid or liquid form, fat contributes to the tender, moist, and smooth mouth feel of baked goods. It also enhances the flavors of other ingredients, as well as contributing its own flavor. In baked goods, such as quick breads, reducing the amount of fat toughens a product. Reduced fat substitutes have less than 80 percent fat, and do not work the same as butter or oil in baked goods. Butter is a solid fat made from cream and has a fat content of at least 80 percent. The remaining 20 percent is water with some milk solids. Butter imparts a good flavor without a greasy mouth feel. In baking, use unsalted butter for total control over the amount of salt you use.

Tip: A baked product in which soft butter is creamed or whipped has a different texture than one with oil or melted butter. Whipped butter, especially butter creamed with sugar, has a network of air bubbles that acts as a raising agent during cooking. The result is a pound-cake-like crumb. A recipe with melted butter has a more traditional muffin or quick bread crumb.

Tip: Butter reaches room temperature in about 20 minutes. Do not microwave to soften cold butter. To soften quickly, cut the butter into small pieces. If your recipe calls for melted butter, make sure it is lukewarm, not hot, before adding it to the rest of the ingredients. Butter warmer than 90° F (32° C) can cook the eggs in the dough, causing clumping.

5. Liquid Fat

I sometimes use liquid oils (safflower, sunflower, canola, and olive) in place of unsalted butter. When I do, it is because oil is more desirable. One big difference is texture of the cake. Oil-based cake is moister, although it may be oilier. Vegetable oils have a fairly neutral taste, while butter has a more interesting flavor. Therefore, a recipe using oil might be blander than one with butter, which is why I add plenty of spices and flavorings.

Tip: Oil is delicate and can spoil. Smell the oil before using. Flavorless oils, such as safflower, sunflower, and canola, should be odorless.

Tip: For baking, use the above light-flavored oils. Olive oils, especially extra-virgin, cold pressed, may be used for a more distinct, less mild flavor.

Tip: To substitute oil for butter, use ⅞ cup (14 tablespoons) oil for 1 cup butter.

6. Gluten-Forming Flours

Because wheat is the most common distributed cereal grain in the world, a reference to flour is generally a reference to wheat flour. These flours provide structure in baked goods. Flour from wheat contains proteins that form gluten. The more protein the flour contains, the higher the gluten and the stronger and more elastic the dough. Different types of wheat flour contain different amounts of the gluten-forming proteins. For instance, hard wheat is high in protein. Soft wheat has less. A strong gluten framework is desirable in yeast breads; but cake, quick bread, and pastry with high protein flour will be tough. Wheat flours I use in baking include stone ground; cake; unbleached all-purpose; and whole wheat.

Stone ground flour is ground between two stones. The nutritious hull and germ of a kernel are usually left in, so the texture is coarser. Other flour is ground between metal rollers, and the hull and germ are removed, so the texture is finer.

Cake flour is soft wheat that is 7.5 percent protein. This lower gluten product has a tender, more crumbly texture that is sometimes desirable in cake.

Unbleached all-purpose flour has a medium protein content of 10.5 percent. This white flour can be used for all types of baking. When using all-purpose flour in place of cake flour, substitute 1 cup minus 2 tablespoons all-purpose flour for 1 cup cake flour.

Whole wheat pastry and bread flours may be substituted for part of the white flour in yeast and quick bread recipes. This high-protein nutritious flour contains the germ and bran as well as the endosperm of the wheat kernel, making it healthier than white. Whole grains have a nut-like quality, a subtle sweetness, and distinct texture and flavor variations. However, a baked product with whole grain is heavier and smaller than one without. For best results, when substituting whole wheat flour for white, use ½ whole wheat and ½ white flour. I use whole wheat pastry flour in my baking. It is made from softer wheat and is much lower in gluten than bread flour. It is also good for pastries and other desserts.

Tip: All flour should be stored in either the refrigerator or freezer for freshness and quality and brought to room temperature before measuring.

Tip: All flour should be remeasured after sifting.

7. Non-Gluten Forming Flours

These flours are gaining in popularity. Because they are made from non-cereal grains, and do not form gluten, they are a favorite ingredient for those with celiac disease. The following are protein-rich, non-gluten grain flours that I use in some of my baking. Some, such as potato flour, arrowroot, and tapioca flour, are also used as starches or thickeners. They soften and lighten the consistency of cakes and breads, while increasing the effectiveness of whatever raising agent you add to the recipe.

Tip: Freeze or refrigerate for freshness and quality, and bring to room temperature before measuring.

Gluten-free, all-purpose flour

Rather than making my own, I use some of the many all-purpose gluten-free flours that are now widely available in markets. For those who want to bake a gluten-free recipe from scratch, refer to the descriptions below for those gluten-free flours and other additives you can use. There are many different recipes for gluten-free flour. Below is one example:

1. Mix 2 cups rice flour, ⅓ cup tapioca flour, ⅔ cup potato starch, and 2 teaspoons xanthan gum in a medium-size bowl.
2. Because this has xanthan gum added, you do not need to add it if a recipe has it listed.

Amaranth flour is gluten-free, and may be combined with another non-grain flour or starch to replace 25% of the flour in recipes.

Cornmeal is coarsely ground dried corn. Corn flour is more finely ground corn. Both taste like corn, and have a rough crumbly texture in baked products. Use unrefined, yellow cornmeal for increased nutrition and a slightly crunchy texture.

Guar gum. See number 19, Guar gum and xantham gum.

Mesquite flour is made from the ground pods of the mesquite tree, which is grown in the southwestern regions of the U.S. and other desert climates worldwide. It has a delicate, distinctive flavor that is naturally sweet and slightly nutty, with a hint of molasses. It is rich in calcium, magnesium, potassium, iron, and zinc, and is purported to be especially good for stabilizing the blood sugar of diabetics. I substitute it for ¼ of the dry ingredients in many of my baking recipes.

Tip: Since mesquite flour is sweet, you might want to cut down slightly on the amount of sugar in the recipe.

Tip: Mesquite flour is distributed to large health food markets throughout the United States and can also be found online.

Tip: This can have a strong taste and result in heavier crumb texture. Therefore, substitute no more than 25% mesquite flour for dry ingredients in a recipe.

Nut meals. See number 11, Nuts and seeds.

Oat bran (flakes) and flour are milled from high protein oat. Oat bran is a nutritious source of soluble fiber and may be substituted for as much as ⅓ wheat flour in baked goods.

Potato flour is usually used in combination with other flours. It has a mild potato taste. ⅝ cup potato flour may be substituted for 1 cup all-purpose flour.

Rice flour. Both brown rice flour and white rice flour may be used in place of wheat in a gluten-free diet. Brown rice flour is made from unpolished brown rice and is more nutritious than white. Brown is best when finely ground, in recipes that can tolerate some grittiness, such as pound cakes and cornbread. White has a less gritty texture than brown rice. Rice flour is not suitable for yeast cookery but can be used for baking biscuits, cakes, and cookies. It tends to absorb more water than wheat flour. Thus, when using rice flour in baking, make adjustments. Do not replace 1-to-1 for wheat flour. Use ⅞ cup of non-waxy rice flour for 1 cup all-purpose flour.

Soy flour is made from ground soybeans and is used primarily to boost protein content. If used in large amounts, it affects the taste of baked goods and causes them to brown quickly. Substitute soy flour for 1 to 2 tablespoons flour for each cup in a recipe.

Tapioca flour is starchy, slightly sweet, white, gluten-free flour derived from the cassava root. Use approximately ¼ to ½ cup in a recipe for sweet breads made with rice or millet flour.

Wheat germ is the germ extracted from wheat and is often substituted for part of the flour in recipes for flavor and fiber. Wheat germ, preferably toasted, can be used in place of up to ⅓ of the flour in a recipe.

Xanthan gum. See number 19, Guar gum and xanthan gum.

8. Dry, Fresh and Frozen Fruit

Dry fruit (apples, apricots, pears, and raisins) enhance the flavor of many baked goods. They are particularly flavorful when reconstituted with liquid.

Place dry fruit in a small bowl and cover with warm water. Set aside for 10 minutes or until fruit is plumped. Drain well and pat dry with a paper towel.

Fresh fruit. Apples and bananas are versatile baking fruit with year-round availability. A great baking apple has a good sweet-tart balance and flesh that does not break down when cooked. Bananas should be ripe for fuller flavor. Although pears may be available much of the year, they are best in the fall season.

Frozen fruit. When fresh fruit is not in season, substitute with unsweetened frozen. Do not defrost prior to use.

Tip: Do not dust frozen fruit with flour.

Tip: Recipes made with frozen fruit rather than fresh take a little longer to cook.

9. Leavening Agents

Baking soda, baking powder, and yeast are chemicals that cause batters to rise when baked. However, it is the baking powder that does the most leavening. Baking soda, on the other hand, is added just to neutralize the acids in the batter and to add tenderness. Yeast is a living organism that requires a warm, moist environment and a food source to grow and thrive. These three agents enlarge the bubbles, which are already present in batter and dough. However, they are not interchangeable.

Baking soda (sodium bicarbonate) produces gas for leavening when combined with an acidic ingredient such as vinegar, lemon juice, or molasses. The volume of quick breads, cakes, and cookies depends largely on how much baking soda is added. If the amount is reduced and not replaced with another leavening agent, the product will have less volume and be heavier. Baking soda has a white, crystalline, solid appearance.

Baking powder contains baking soda and the right amount of acid to react with it. Baking powder is available as single-acting and double-acting. Single-acting powders are activated by moisture, so you must bake recipes with this product immediately after mixing. Double-acting powders react in two phases and can stand for a while before baking. Baking powder is dry, white, and has the consistency of powder.

Tip: Batters made with baking soda should be baked soon after mixing for best results, because the leavening starts to work as soon as the wet and dry ingredients are combined.

Tip: Use baking soda and baking powder within four months of opening, or freeze for up to one year. To make corn-free powder, shake 4 tablespoons each of arrowroot powder and cream of tartar, plus 2 tablespoons baking soda in a covered jar.

Baker's (or brewer's) yeast is used as a leavening agent in baking and is the reason bread is fluffy and light. Yeast ferments the flour in the dough, releasing carbon dioxide into the bread, causing it to rise. Yeast is available in many forms. Compressed, active dry, instant, and rapid rise are most common for home baking. Most forms of yeast can be used interchangeably.

10. Liquids: Juice, Milk, Buttermilk, Soy Milk, and Nut Milk

Liquid is necessary in baked goods. It helps carry flavor throughout the product, forms gluten bonds and reacts with the starch in proteins for a strong but light structure. Liquid also behaves like steam during baking, acting as a leavening agent and contributing to the tenderness of a product.

Juice may be used as the liquid and sweetener in a recipe. Because fruit juices are acidic, they are probably best used in baked products that have baking soda as an ingredient.

Milk contributes water and nutrients to baked goods. It increases browning and adds flavor.

Buttermilk is ideal in baking because it has no fat and acts much like whole milk.

Tip: Make buttermilk by combining 1 tablespoon white vinegar or fresh-squeezed lemon juice with enough of any kind of milk to equal 1 cup. Let stand for 5 minutes, until milk begins to curdle. See also #18, Vinegar.

Tip: When substituting buttermilk for milk, you must change the amount of baking soda and baking powder. Because of the higher acid content in buttermilk, you will usually need less baking soda or baking powder. For each cup of buttermilk used instead of milk, use 2 teaspoons less baking powder and ½ teaspoon more baking soda.

Soy milk and **nut milks** are silky and work well in gluten-free baking. They are ideal for people who are lactose-intolerant, galactosemic, allergic to milk protein, or choose not to consume dairy for ethical reasons. Because they are lactose-free, they are often a good substitute for cow's milk, providing a substantial source of protein and a fair supply of calcium. When using soy milk in place of cow's milk, there may be a subtle difference in taste, color, and texture in some recipes.

Soy milk will not alter any other ratios of your baked goods. Cakes, muffins, and cookies can be made with soy milk.

Tip: Substitute soy and nut milks for cow's in recipes on a 1-to-1 ratio.

Tip: Soy milk will add a variant nutty "soy" flavor to your baked goods. Add extracts such as almond or vanilla to overpower and virtually cancel out the subtle soy flavor.

Tip: Choose the right soy milk for each recipe. Try flavored, unflavored, sweetened, and unsweetened varieties of soy milk. If you are baking a sweet product, make sure to balance the sweetness of the milk with less sugar than called for in the recipe.

Use the flavors to your advantage; for instance, if you are making a vanilla cake, use vanilla-flavored soy milk. Plain, lightly sweetened soy milk is best for breads and salty baked goods. Sweetened soy works best in puddings, cupcakes, and other desserts.

Tip: To make lactose-free buttermilk, mix 1 cup soy or nut milk with 1 teaspoon apple cider vinegar, and let sit for 5 minutes.

11. Nuts and Seeds

I think of nuts as large, dense, edible seeds, and seeds as the smaller ones that require more work to actually eat in their natural state.

Nuts are mostly a good source of protein and healthy fats and, unless you have nut allergies, can be eaten in moderation without problem. (In baking, you can often, but not always, substitute one kind of nut and/or nut meal for another.)

Tip: Nuts are not always interchangeable in a recipe because they vary in oil content and flavor. It is preferable to grind them in a nut grinder. If you use a food processor or blender, grind the nuts quickly and evenly, so as not to extract the oil.

Tip: Ground nuts can be used in flourless cakes or to complement other flours.

Tip: Once packaged nuts are open, be sure to store in an airtight container or sealed baggie with air squeezed out in a cool, dry, dark place (ideally in the refrigerator or freezer) and use within 3 months. For maximum shelf life, avoid exposing nuts to humidity.

Nut meals are ground from whole nuts, and are grittier and oilier than nut flours, which are ground from the cake that remains after the oils are pressed from nuts. Nut meals add moisture and a rich nutty taste to baked items. But, because they lack the gluten that baked goods need for rising, I do not substitute more than ¼ wheat flour with nut. (Tortes are an exception in which I use all nut meal.) More eggs (and whipped egg whites) are usually required when baking with nut meal for more structure. Nut meal is widely available in stores. However, if you want to make your own, grind toasted nuts in a nut mill until it has the consistency of cornmeal, or in a food processor fitted with a steel blade. Nut flours include almond, pecan, walnut, hazelnut, filbert and chestnut.

Tip: If you decide to make your own nut meal, keep in mind that it is difficult to keep the nut meal from turning into nut butter. It helps to freeze the nuts before grinding, to use the pulse setting on the processor, and to add any sugar in the recipe to the nuts to help absorb the oils.

Seeds: pepita (shelled pumpkin seeds), sesame, and sunflower

Pepita (pumpkin seeds) are slightly sweet and rich in nutrition. However, they are full of calories and fat, so they should be eaten in moderation.

Sesame seeds are rich in quality vitamins and minerals. Sesame seeds are small, almost oblate in shape with pleasant nutty flavor and high oil content. Store them in a cool, dark place, such as a refrigerator. Properly stored, dry seeds generally stay fresh for several months.

Sunflower seeds are the nutritious kernels from the hard-shelled seeds found in the head of the sunflower. In fact, they are not really seeds at all, but the fruit of the sunflower. Sunflower seeds taste great and are highly nutritious.

12. Rolled Oats

Rolled oats are the whole grain of oats flattened by rollers, and are available in a variety of cuts. The most common for baking is old fashioned (regular) because of its substantial chewy texture and pleasant nutty flavor. The old fashioned are, also, more nutritious and great for baking. Use certified gluten-free oats in gluten-free recipes. This designation guarantees that the oats are harvested and processed in a wheat-free environment.

13. Sea Salt

Salt strengthens gluten and enhances the flavors and sweetness of other ingredients in food. In yeast breads, it helps moderate the effect of the yeast so that the bread does not rise too quickly. If salt is omitted or reduced, other spices or flavorings in the recipe should be increased slightly. I prefer to use sea salt rather than table salt. **Sea salt** is an all-purpose salt that is harvested from evaporated seawater and receives little or no processing. Table salt is processed and has a sharp taste. Because table salt has very fine crystals, a single teaspoon of table salt contains more salt than a tablespoon of kosher or sea salt.

14. Sour Cream

Sour cream tenderizes and softens baked goods. It is made from adding lactic acid-producing bacteria to cream to produce a slightly tart, thick sour cream. Sour cream is high in fat and calories. Two tablespoons of regular has 60 calories; low-fat has 40, and fat-free has only 25. The type you use depends upon the texture and outcome you want. For example, if you're looking for a creamier, moister baked product, use full-fat sour cream. Reduced-fat is healthier, but it still contains a significant number of calories and amount of fat. If you want your baked goods to be lower in fat and calories, use fat-free sour cream or low-fat or fat-free yogurt instead.

Tip: Although sealed sour cream may be stored for up to 2 weeks beyond the sell-by date, it loses flavor as it ages. Pink or green scum indicates spoilage.

Tip: Sour cream should always be kept refrigerated.

Tip: If you notice any liquid separation in sour cream after it has been open, either pour off the liquid or stir it in.

15. Spices: Allspice, Cardamom, Cinnamon, Cloves, Coriander, Ginger, Nutmeg, and Pumpkin

Tip: While ground spices are fine for baking, they do lose their fresh flavor when ground. For the most robust flavor, it is hard to improve upon grinding your own. I have one coffee grinder that I use exclusively for this purpose. Instead, you may put the whole spice in a plastic bag and grind with a hammer. Whole spices last about one year stored in an airtight container in a cool, dark place (never near a hot stove or vent), 6 months longer than the ground form. Extend the shelf life of spices by storing them in the refrigerator.

Allspice has a combined flavor of cinnamon, nutmeg, and cloves with a hint of juniper and peppercorn. Jamaica is the principle distributor of allspice worldwide. It is available in ground form as well as whole berries.

Cardamom is an aromatic spice indigenous to South India, and is now grown in tropical areas, including Sri Lanka, the islands of the Pacific, and Central America. It has a strong, unique warm, spicy-sweet taste and can be purchased in pods, seeds, or ground.

Cinnamon is the brown bark of the cinnamon tree and is available in a dried tubular form or as ground powder. There are two varieties of cinnamon, Chinese and Ceylonese. Chinese is the least expensive and most popular in the United States.

Both have a fragrant, sweet, warm taste. Cinnamon has a long history, both as a spice and as a medicine.

Tip: The sticks can be stored for longer, but the ground powder has a stronger flavor. Smell the cinnamon to make sure that it has a sweet smell, a characteristic reflecting that it is fresh. If it does not, discard it. Ground cinnamon will keep for about 6 months, while cinnamon sticks will stay fresh for about 1 year when properly stored.

Clove dates back more than 2,500 years, to Ancient China. It has a warming, sweet, and spicy taste that complements many sweet breads and muffins. Clove can be bought whole or ground. For baking, it should be ground. As with many spices, freshly ground has more flavor and aroma than clove bought ground. In addition to cooking, clove has many medicinal uses.

Coriander spice is a dried fruit containing a few true seeds that are ground for baking. It is best known as an ingredient in baked goods, and has a subtle flavor that is warm and spicy with a slight hint of the fresh cilantro leaves and a complex aromatic scent that is soothingly warm, nutty, and slightly fruity.

Ginger spice is a buff-colored ground spice made from the dried root of ginger. It has a warm, spicy-sweet bouquet and is common in baking.

Nutmeg, as well as mace, is a spice from the fruit of the tall evergreen nutmeg tree, indigenous to the Spice Islands of Indonesia. (Mace is the dried reddish lacy covering that surrounds the seed kernel from which the nutmeg comes.) It is used powdered and is best when grated fresh. It has a sweet, spicy nutty taste that complements many baked goods, especially those with pumpkin.

Pumpkin spice is a combination of aromatic spices used to enhance the blandness of pumpkin recipes.

Tip: Pumpkin spice may be purchased premixed or made by combining ½ teaspoon ground cinnamon, ¼ teaspoon ground ginger, ⅛ teaspoon ground nutmeg, and ⅛ teaspoon ground allspice. Proportions may be changed to suit your taste.

16. Dry Sweeteners

Sugar is a highly processed form of sugar beet or sugar cane plant extracts. Sucrose, the technical name for table sugar, cane sugar, or white sugar, comes in powdered and granulated forms. It adds sweetness, and holds moisture in baked products. It also prevents gluten from forming, and contributes to browning, although reducing the sugar content by more than ⅓ can cause a loss of these characteristics. When sugar crystals are cut into solid fats, like butter, they help form the structure of a baked product. That is why the first step in many baking recipes is to mix the butter and sugar together.

Brown sugar is sucrose that gets its color from the addition of molasses, obtained predominantly from sugar cane and not beet sugar. Natural brown sugar (raw sugar) is a brown sugar produced from the first crystallization of the sugar cane. There is more molasses in natural brown sugar, and some of these have specific characteristics and names, such as Turbinado, Muscovado, and Demerara sugar. A recipe calling for brown sugar usually refers to light brown sugar. Dark brown, which holds more moisture than light, should be used only when specified. Dark brown will yield a deeper, more caramel flavor than light sugar.

Tip: The darker the sugar, the more moisture it holds.

Tip: Over time, the moisture in brown sugar evaporates and the sugar hardens. To fix this, you need to put the moisture back. There are a number of ways to restore it to its original silky-smooth state, and to keep it soft and flavorful. My favorite is to place the sugar in a bowl in the microwave alongside a small cup of water. Cook for one minute on high. Check and continue to microwave in 30-second increments until soft. (Warning: The sugar will be hot, so handle carefully.) When it is soft, I use two methods to keep it that way. After opening, I store most of it in a plastic bag in the freezer. I also store some in an airtight container with a small terra cotta "brown sugar preserver" that I remoisten every few months.

17. Liquid Sweeteners

A natural sugar liquid sweetener (such as agave nectar, honey, maple syrup, and molasses) may be substituted for a dry sweetener, but doing so may change the balance of dry to wet ingredients in a recipe. Most recipes will need to be adjusted. In general, when converting:

Replace each cup of sugar with ⅔ cup of natural liquid sweetener,

Reduce other liquids in the recipe by about the same proportion, and

Slightly increase the amount of dry ingredients, adding extra flour or ingredients with other flavors and textures such as wheat germ or fine-ground nuts.

Increase the thickening agent, such as arrowroot, cornstarch, or tapioca flour, slightly to compensate for added liquid in a recipe.

Tip: Always dissolve arrowroot and cornstarch in a teaspoon or more of cold liquid before using.

Agave nectar is a sweetener made from the Blue Agave plant. The taste of agave nectar is comparable, though not identical, to honey. Blue agave comes in light and dark versions. The lighter, which can taste like maple syrup, is milder tasting than the dark. Agave has a thin, light consistency.

Honey from bees that feed on specific plants have unique flavors. Use a light-flavored variety for baking. Honey has an indefinite shelf life. Store it in a tightly covered container, in a cool location away from direct sunlight. If it becomes cloudy (crystallizes), bring it back to its original state by warming it on a low heat or in the microwave. Maple syrup can be substituted in equal portions, or use ½ honey, ½ maple syrup in recipes.

Maple syrup is made from the sap of the sugar from maple trees, whose starch is converted to sugar between winter and spring. This viscous amber liquid with its characteristic earthy sweet taste can be used as a delicately flavored sugar substitute. Canada and the United States produce almost all of the world's maple syrup, and each has its own classification system. In general, the subtler flavor of light amber (and Grade A syrups) is considered the premier type, meant for eating. The dark, thicker, more maple-flavored (and Grade B syrups) are generally only used for cooking or baking, where their flavors may shine through. Honey can be used in equal proportions, or use ½ honey, ½ maple syrup in recipes.

Molasses is a sugar syrup byproduct of the sugar refining process. It imparts a dark color and strong caramel flavor to baked foods. It is not as sweet as sugar, so when using molasses in place of sugar, use 1-⅓ cups molasses for 1 cup sugar and reduce the amount of other liquids in the recipe by 5 tablespoons. Because molasses is more acidic than sugar, add ½ teaspoon baking soda for each cup of molasses substituted for sugar. Molasses has a strong flavor, so use it sparingly in combination with other sweeteners. Replace no more than ½ the sugar called for in the recipe with molasses.

18. Vinegar

Rather than keep a quart of buttermilk in the refrigerator, I mostly make it myself with any type of milk and an acid. The main consideration for preparing a substitute for buttermilk is that it must have an acid component. The lactic acid in buttermilk is responsible for its characteristic flavor, leavening power, and texture. I tend to use white vinegar, but you may substitute apple cider vinegar, rice vinegar, or fresh-squeezed lemon juice. For 1 cup buttermilk, place 1 tablespoon vinegar or lemon juice in a liquid measuring cup. Then add enough milk to bring the liquid up to the 1-cup line. Let stand for 5 minutes, or until it starts to curdle. Use what you need. See also #10, Liquids.

19. Guar Gum and Xantham Gum

These are used in gluten-free baking to bind the gluten-free ingredients. Without them, most gluten-free baked goods would be dry and crumbly, and would fall apart. **Guar gum** comes from the seed of a bean-like plant. Because it is high in soluble fiber, it is sometimes associated with gastrointestinal upset. **Xanthan gum** is a corn-based, fermented, natural bacterium. Those with sensitivity to corn might avoid xanthan. Too much guar can result in heavy, stringy baked products and too much xanthan in ones that are heavy, gummy, or even slimy. Both should be measured precisely. A reliable tip for using them in gluten-free cake, muffin and quick bread recipes is to add ½ to ¾ teaspoon per 1 cup of gluten-free flour. (Note: Xanthan gum is much more expensive than Guar gum.)

20. Yogurt

Thick Greek, whole milk, low or nonfat, and soy yogurts are great substitutes for sour cream in baking. Yogurt cuts the fat and adds a creamy texture and tenderness. Plus, it's packed with protein and calcium. Substitute yogurt cup-for-cup for sour cream in recipes.

21. Zest

Zest is the outer layer of the rind of a fruit. Orange and lemon zests are the most popular. Scrape the zest, which contains oils, from the rind and use it as a flavoring in many quick breads.

Altitude Baking

ALTITUDE AFFECTS BAKING. Most recipes are developed for use at sea level, and work up to around 3,500 feet. Above that, they may need some tweaking. Unfortunately, there are no perfect guidelines for baking in high altitudes, as every recipe is different depending on the ingredients and the exact altitude. Typically, recipes can benefit by slight additions or reductions of one or more products, or by altering baking time or temperature. The best way to adjust for high altitude is on a per-recipe basis.

All the recipes in **Baking Breakfast** are based on cooking in my Tucson, Arizona, home, which is 2,600 feet above sea level. Because high-altitude baking is a complex subject, there are many Internet sites with guidelines. A set of publications from the Colorado State University Extension Resource Center (877.692.9358 or http://www.ext.colostate.edu/pubs/pubs.html#nutr_high) and the King Arthur Flour web site (http://www.kingarthurflour.com/recipe/high-altitude-baking.html) are two outstanding resources. The below chart is a general guide to baking at high altitude.

Changes When Baking in High Altitude	
What to Change	How to Change
Oven Temperature	Increase 15-25°F.
Baking Time	Decrease 5-8 minutes per 30 minutes of baking time.
Liquid	Increase 1 to 2 tablespoons at 3,000 feet. For each additional 1,000, increase 1-½ teaspoons more. Depending upon the recipe, you can use additional eggs as part of this liquid.
Sweetener, dry	Decrease by 1 tablespoon per cup.
Flour	At 3,500 feet, add 1 tablespoon per recipe. For each additional 1,500 feet, add 1 more tablespoon.

Measurement Conversion Charts

I HAVE INCLUDED FAHRENHEIT AND CENTIGRADE oven temperatures for all my recipes. However, most measurements are in American Standard volumes and weights such as: ounces, pounds, cups, tablespoons, and teaspoons. For those readers who are more comfortable using Metric measurements, I have included the following chart that has many common baking conversion measurements. (Metric amounts are the nearest equivalents.) This chart is preceded by a list of some basic baking American Standard conversions.

Common American Standard Conversions

1 tablespoon = 3 teaspoons = ½ ounce

4 tablespoons = ¼ cup = 2 ounces

8 tablespoons = ½ cup = 4 ounces

⅓ cup = 5 tablespoons plus one teaspoon

16 ounces = 1 pint = 1 pound

Volume Measurement (fluid)	
American Standard	Metric ml=milliliter
1 teaspoon	5 ml
1 tablespoon	15 ml
¼ cup	60 ml
1 cup	240 ml or ¼ liter
1 pint	480 ml
4 cups or 1 quart, approximately	1 liter

Weight Measurement (dry)		
American Standard	Metric g=gram kg=kilogram	
1 ounce	28 g	
¼ pound	114 g	
2.2 pounds	1 kg	
Flour, all-purpose:	sifted	unsifted
1 tablespoon	8 g	
¼ cup	30 g	
½ cup	60 g	
1 cup (4.75 ounces unsifted)	110 g	136 g
Flour, whole wheat pastry:	unsifted	
1 cup (5.55 ounces, unsifted)	156 g	
Butter:		
1 tablespoon	15 g	
¼ cup	55 g	
1 stick (½ cup or ¼ pound)	115 g	
Nuts:		
1 cup	155 g	
1 cup almond meal (3.45 oz)	96 g	
Sugar, granulated:		
1 tablespoon	15 g	
¼ cup	55 g	
1 cup	225 g	
Sugars, brown packed:		
1 tablespoon	12 g	
¼ cup	55 g	
1 cup	200 g	

Afterword

By George Berkowitz
Founder and former chair, Legal Sea Foods
February 2010

EARLY IN 2010 I RECEIVED a letter from my niece, Jill Berkowitz Provan, my brother Leonard's daughter and the author of this book. She asked me to compose a dedication to a cookbook she was writing in honor of her father. When I received Jill's letter, it had been years since we had communicated. Hearing from her stoked my memory and I was overwhelmed by images of growing up with Leonard in the Mattapan and Newton suburbs of Boston.

Our father, Harry, was the proprietor of Legal Cash Market in Inman Square; I later opened Legal Sea Foods next door, which I ran until passing the business on to my son Roger in 1992. Harry was always smiling, and he loved the little children who prowled the aisles with their parents. I never saw him angry. "It's just as easy to be nice," he often said. During the Depression, he proved his point by giving food to customers who had no money. "Pay me when you can," became a favorite expression.

As I look back, I see that Leonard was much like our father, who was a great mentor for both of us. Leonard also smiled constantly, was very ethical, and loved children. I always admired him. At the age of 14, when Leonard was attending the University of Maine and playing varsity football, I would walk around the house singing the "University of Maine Stein Song." I was so proud of him.

After graduating from college, Leonard became a lieutenant commander in the Navy, serving on the seaplane tender USS Albermarle. During World War II, the Albemarle plied the North Atlantic looking for German U-boats. When the war ended, Leonard and I worked at Legal Cash Market together. (The market got that name because Harry gave Legal Stamps to customers—forerunner to the better-known S&H Green Stamps—with every purchase.) Legal Cash Market sold only the finest: The meats were prime grade and the vegetables were freshly picked, supplied by a farmer every morning.

After working with our father, Leonard worked in the food business for many years before finally going out on his own. Soon after he moved to Miami, he became head meat consultant for the Marriott Corporation, and for the American Angus and Lamb Associations. He was a founding professor in the School of Hospitality and Tourism Management at Florida International University. These are but a few of the jobs he held during his professional career, during which time many awards were bestowed upon him.

Leonard was a wonderful husband to his wife Thelma and father to his three daughters. He was a great son to our mother, who lived to be 99 years old. Even though a caretaker lived with her, Leonard cooked and delivered meals for her regularly. He called her every evening to say good night and to "make sure everything is OK."

Leonard passed away in 1991, and though many years have gone by, I think of him often. I am proud to claim Leonard Irving Berkowitz as my brother, and proud that his daughter has written this extraordinary testament to our family and food—one could not exist without the other.

Index

A

B

D

E

F

G

H

J

L

M

N

O

P

R

S

T

U

V

Jill Berkowitz Provan was born in Boston, Massachusetts, into a family of food lovers, cooks, and restaurateurs. For some family members, cooking was a serious hobby; for others, it was a livelihood. Jill grew up eating wonderful food made with high-quality ingredients, and this shaped her life.

In **Baking Breakfast,** Jill has put her passion for baking to work. She has created dozens of inventive and delectable recipes. In place of traditional ingredients, she often substitutes healthy alternatives, such as whole wheat flour, nut meals, maple syrup, and agave nectar, many of which have just recently become widely available at affordable prices.

Made in the USA
San Bernardino, CA
26 March 2018